media

MANUAL

make-up, hair and costume for film and television

media

Series editor: Peter Ward

MANUAL

media

MANUAL

make-up, hair and costume for film and television

jan musgrove

Focal Press

Focal Press
An imprint of Elsevier
Linacre House, Jordan Hill, Oxford OX2 8DP
200 Wheeler Road, Burlington MA 01803

First published 2003

British Library Cataloguing in Publication Data
Musgrove, Jan
  Make-up, hair and costume for film and television
  1. Television   2. Costume   3. Theatrical makeup
  I. Title
  791.4'5'026

Library of Congress Cataloguing in Publication Data
Musgrove, Jan.
  Make-up, hair and costume for film and television/Jan Musgrove.
  p. cm – (Media manual)
  Includes bibliographical references.
  ISBN 0-240-51660-5 (alk. paper)
  1. Television makeup.   2. Costume.   I. Title.   II. Media manuals.

PN1992.8.M36M86 2003
791.45'027–dc21   2003040832

ISBN 0 240 51660 5

For information on all Focal Press publications visit our website at:
www.focalpress.com

Typeset by Keyword Typesetting Services Ltd
Printed and bound in Great Britain by Biddles Ltd

Contents

Acknowledgements

Thanks to friends and colleagues for their help and encouragement in compiling this manual, particularly to the following:

Make-up: Carole Bernard, Judy Courtney, Sarah Piper
Hairdressing and wig-making: Barbie Burrows
Costume: Kim Burns, Barbara Rutter
Lighting: Bill Lee
Cameras: Peter Ward
Production: Joanna Gollins
Proofreading and formatting: Christine Courtney

Studio photographs courtesy of the Short Course Unit (NSCTP) at the National Film and Television School.

Working in film and video

There are many aspects of media work that may require make-up and wardrobe facilities. These include:

- feature films;
- video production;
- film production for television;
- advertising;
- pop promotions;
- corporate work;
- education and training.

Depending on the film stock and cameras used, picture quality does vary and it is necessary to be aware of the differences. For television productions 16 mm film stock is used and for the cinema 35 mm stock. The latter gives greater detail and clarity; what would be acceptable for TV may not be acceptable on a huge cinema screen.

As the object of having make-up, hairstyling and wardrobe facilities is to enhance the picture quality, all productions would benefit from having them, but budget restrictions mean that very often small productions must manage without. The use of cameras and lighting can produce hard and unsympathetic pictures. This is often noticeable even to the general public, when we see people looking tired, men who look as though they haven't shaved for several days and jackets that cause the camera to 'strobe'.

Make-up, hair and wardrobe are service departments, their aim being to help create pictures that are pleasing to the eye, or to help create an impression or atmosphere that is correct for the production needs. This may simply be achieved by correcting any problems that may exist, or by creating a disguise or character to tell a story. Every production has different needs, and therefore a wide range of knowledge and skills is required to cater for whatever is expected, and very often for what is unexpected.

These particular departments are also expected to create a calm and relaxing environment for artists and members of the public appearing on camera. They are the last ports of call before the individual gives a performance or interview, and there will be considerable anxiety. It is important for the departments' staff to stay relaxed and unruffled under extreme pressure, whether that comes from an anxious artist or from a floor assistant demanding the artist be ready in two minutes!

The skills and knowledge required in each department are similar in all areas of media work and staff are able to work in any area. The one major difference in working practice is in the hairdressing department. For television and video work, make-up and hair are both done by the make-up artist. This is probably because when television first started the hairdressing requirements were fairly basic – making sure the hair was smooth and tidy. Stray hairs catch the strong lights and can be distracting. In cinema and photographic work, make-up and

Final touches to the set on 'A Tale of Pig Robinson'

hairdressing are generally separate departments. Make-up artists do not touch the hair at all and qualified hairdressers are employed for hairdressing alone. In the theatre, wigmakers are responsible for hairdressing.

One of the most challenging aspects of working in television and film is getting the work! There is plenty of work available but many people trying to get it. It takes courage and determination, but offers a very varied and exciting career.

Television

The television industry internationally has a vast turnover, and provides millions of people with information, education and entertainment. The viewer, however, does not see the complexities and the wide range of skills involved behind the camera. It is important to recognize the need in all departments for training to ensure professional and skilful work. Particularly with the provision of make-up, hair and wardrobe, it would be easy to feel that it was possible to bluff your way through a production. However, with the huge expense of making programmes, budgeting is a major factor and every minute lost due to lack of knowledge and expertise costs the production money. This, of course, raises the question of whether the production can afford to employ make-up, hair or wardrobe staff at all. It used to be the case that large TV studios employed permanent staff and offered sufficient training, but now few of them do and the employment is predominantly freelance.

For make-up staff there is a difference between TV and film. For much TV work the make-up and hair requirements are simple and straightforward. It was probably for this reason that the make-up artist was also expected to do any hairdressing required. When television began to produce entertainment, especially period drama, the make-up artist had to learn appropriate hairdressing skills.

Today, make-up and hair are still one department, and their skills include working with wigs and facial hair. As hairdressing takes longer to learn and become proficient at, it is helpful if hairdressing skills are developed first. Make-

Working in a studio

up staff have continued to add to their skills, as in the use of special effects materials including prosthetics.

The make-up or costume personnel need to be very adaptable as they may be working alone or with others, and their contract may be for a day or it may be for several weeks, depending on the production.

A make-up or costume designer, when working on a drama production, will be employed before filming or recording starts, to read scripts, meet artists and to buy or hire anything required. Any other make-up or costume personnel will join the production when filming or recording starts, or may only work on days when guest artists or extra background artists appear.

Production companies and designers or heads of departments like to build up a nucleus of people with whom they like to work. Networking is extremely important, not ony to get to know what work is available, but to become known to those who might employ you.

The main benefit in working in television is that the work is mainly short-term contracts, usually daily contracts, sometimes weekly, and only on longer drama productions might a contract be as long as three months. This does allow for a more settled home life and some chance of organizing a social life.

Television

Cinema

As cinema demands top quality pictures, more time and money are available for make-up and hairdressing, and the departments are separate. The hairdresser has to undertake extra training to be able to work with wigs, although any facial hair is dealt with by the make-up department.

However, as television make-up artists were required to do hairdressing as well as make-up, it became apparent that perhaps a good way to work was to have one make-up artist look after one actor or actress. This cuts down on time needed to move from one department to another, and many actors and actresses prefer contact with fewer people. Increasingly, smaller film productions are now working in this way.

The training, work, knowledge and skills of the make-up and costume artists are the same for cinema as for television, but perhaps have more intensity. The demands are greater, from the point of view of the accountant with enormous budget constraints to the increased commitment needed from the staff.

A make-up, hair or costume designer is employed before the filming starts to do the necessary research, designing, buying and making, and to calculate how many other staff members will be needed. There may be camera tests to do, and a script breakdown and continuity notes to make. There is also work to be done at the end of a production, as clothes and wigs must be returned to hire companies.

Filming can take you to many parts of the world

For other make-up and costume staff working on the film, the contract would be for the duration of the film shoot, whether that is completed on time or takes longer than expected. More staff are hired on a daily basis when there are additional guest artists and/or background artists, often known as 'extras'.

It is expected that about two and a half minutes of film will be shot per day, which means that an average film will take three months to make. Film production units usually work a six-day week, but it is not unusual to work seven days a week if problems occur. Hours are long and often contracted into a payment deal, overtime only being paid outside of these hours. It is not unusual to work for six days a week, fourteen hours a day, for six months. Needless to say, this kind of commitment does not help family or social life! However, working in this way, so closely with others, creates an environment of its own. You will be part of a production team under constraints, which makes for special bonding and, hopefully, its own social life. It can be a hard, but memorable experience.

Cinema

The working environment is not always glamorous!

Theatre

Sadly, most theatres do not employ make-up staff, as it would be good to keep the tradition of theatre make-up alive. Artists are expected to do their own make-up. Most theatres also have only limited costume staff, mainly for general maintenance of costumes. There are now, however, more productions requiring special costume and make-up. Designers are contracted to do this work. They will not usually stay with the production throughout its run.

Theatres that do employ permanent and freelance staff are, of course, the homes of such companies as opera and the Royal Shakespeare Company. There may be a permanent wig manager or make-up manager whilst other staff are seasonal, usually employed for eight months per year.

For theatre work the make-up department is split again and hairdressing is undertaken by the wig department because of the large number of wigs made and used. The wig manager may even be responsible for the make-up department as well as the wig department. The number of staff is kept to a minimum and artists are expected to do things for themselves wherever possible.

Every production will have a budget for each department and the designers will plan accordingly, taking into account what is available in stock. Costume is a major part of theatre work and it is likely that most costumes are specially made. Large companies may employ their own tailors, cutters and stitchers or sewers. There may even be finishers for buttons and trims. Although things are improving, tight budgets mean low wages and the hours are long and unsociable, usually from mid-morning until late at night.

The principles of theatre make-up and hairdressing are the same as for other media, though the effects should be seen from the back of the theatre. This means that some traditional make-up effects can be used and the application of the make-up can be considerably heavier. It must be remembered that theatres use more coloured gels on the lights, which will have an effect on the make-up used. All this adds to the atmosphere of the theatre. Only when a theatre production is being televised would a serious problem arise. In this case, it is likely that a TV make-up artist would be brought in to oversee the production.

As with any drama, rehearsals take place over a period of time before the production goes into the theatre. There may be a few days or a week of rehearsals in the theatre itself to set up moves on the stage and lighting. Then there is a final Dress Rehearsal when all design staff can see their work and make any final small adjustments.

After the Dress Rehearsal, that night and the following morning, the costumes and wigs are checked and prepared for the cast for the next performance, the First Night. This pattern of working will continue until the end of the production or the season.

Rehearsals take place for 'La Traviata'

Photography

Photographic work is done for television and film shoots, but the genre also includes stills photography for advertising, etc. The basic skills are the same, but in stills photography greater care is taken with every detail and aspect of the picture.

When doing a photographic session for television or film, the make-up and costume staff looking after the artist will also attend the session and, having done their work, will stand by for every photo to make sure nothing is out of place. Sometimes the photographer will come to the TV studios or film location, but usually the photographs will be taken in a photographic studio where the lighting can be regulated.

Make-up, hair and costume staff will, of course, work closely with the photographer. A photograph is taken first with a Polaroid or digital camera and the resulting picture is used to check details by both the photographer and the make-up and costume personnel. It is slow and painstaking work.

There may not be much in the way of a make-up room or separate dressing rooms, which is why many photographic make-up artists learn to make up the artist looking directly at the face, unlike film and television make-up artists who work looking in a mirror. With stills photography a make-up artist and a hairdresser will be required.

Training as a make-up artist for photographic work concentrates on perfecting every aspect of the application of make-up. It is the one area of the business

Preparing for a photo shoot

that does not necessitate training in other aspects such as character or special effects make-up. However, as a make-up artist this restricts your work to stills photography alone.

Fashion photography covers several areas:

- *portrait work* – for people being photographed for magazines, etc.;
- *advertising* – magazine advertisements for cosmetics, clothes and other products;
- *catalogue photographs* – mainly for clothes catalogues;
- *fashion shows* – make-up for cat-walk models, showing designer clothes.

Some of the work particularly requires speed, looking after several models in a short time, such as fashion shows and catalogue work. For advertising shoots, make-up, hair and costume need to be of a very high standard so time is allowed in these instances to perfect the work.

For someone wanting to work in photography, an interest in fashion is essential and a portfolio of work must be built up.

Working as a stylist

In recent years, artists who travel a lot, such as popular musicians and some film celebrities, have decided it works well to have the same person to take care of all their make-up, hairdressing and costume needs; preferably someone who can travel with them. This enables the stylist to get to know the artist very well, their good points, their weak points and their taste in clothes. It saves a lot of time and anxiety for the artist.

A quick rest amidst the chaos and clutter of a fashion show

Working as staff

It used to be the case that broadcasting organizations employed their own staff and provided ongoing support and training. Unfortunately there are very few organizations that do so now. Those that do employ permanent staff may not provide training. The variety of work staff do may be limited by the type of work the organization does, e.g. studios that broadcast only news items.

The advantages of being permanently employed are numerous:

- although the financial reward is less than for freelance work, it is continuous. There is no anxiety over what you may or may not earn each month;
- holidays, sick pay and a pension are paid;
- any expenses away from base are paid for and staff are covered by insurance;
- equipment and materials are provided, although these may be sparse and certainly every make-up artist will have their own materials with which they prefer to work.

The disadvantages of being employed are related to the priorities of the organization. They would wish staff to be used efficiently and economically, which may mean long hours and little choice in the kind of work you do.

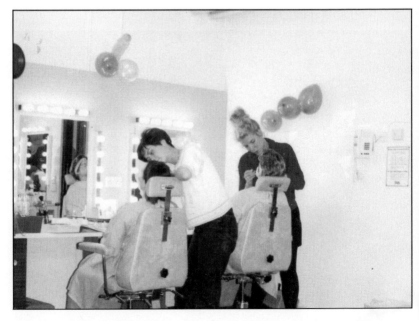

A busy time in the make-up room

There may be restricted choice in the field of work anyway, leaving no chance to develop and use creative skills.

Contract work guarantees a certain amount of work, maybe over weeks or months. Some of the advantages of staff payments are shared but, because the company provides the place of work and the materials, you will be employed on a Pay-As-You-Earn basis. When the contract ends there is the chance to move on. This provides advantages for the company too, of course. You may not wish to move on! However, if the contract has been for a busy production for many months, a well-earned rest will be needed.

There are many people who prefer to stay in employment or contract work if they can because, in spite of its limitations, it offers security, peace of mind and the sense of belonging. They like the continuity of the work and the people.

Working as freelance

As times have changed and companies have had to review their financial commitments, the workforce has now become predominantly freelance. This means that nothing can be taken for granted.

Freelance work offers all the benefits of self-employment, if you are the type of person who sees them as benefits! It requires good business management skills in organizing tax and insurance, purchasing equipment and, of course, getting work. This is where many people falter as it requires the ability to 'sell yourself' – perseverance and a nature that doesn't become easily despondent. This is considered a glamorous business and many a young person's dream. The demand for work greatly outstrips what is available. Even for experienced, skilled make-up, hair and costume personnel work is not guaranteed. It is not uncommon for freelance people to have other interests or work that they can fall back on in between their contracts.

People who enjoy freelance work like the wide variety of work this business offers and the constant change of location and people. However, working as a freelance person means taking much more responsibility for your own business affairs.

- **Insurance:** this is the major necessity, public liability insurance being of utmost importance. As products are used on skin and hair, adequate insurance for all risks must be taken out. The insurance will need to cover normal business items such as computers, mobile phones and car, but also for keeping your equipment at home. There are insurance companies who understand the nature of the business and will provide the correct cover. Details can usually be obtained from union offices.
- **Equipment:** freelance staff have to provide their own materials and equipment. As they have to be prepared for every type of production and every eventuality, this means a considerable outlay. It also means carrying this amount of equipment to each location. As well as hardware such as tongs, hairdryers and irons, there are consumable goods, particularly for make-up artists, in the form of powders, foundations, etc. If a considerable amount is used for a production, there will be a budget provided for this, otherwise the cost of replacement is part of being self-employed.
- **Finding work:** this will entail talking to and meeting people in the business and having a good attitude and approach to the job. Your CV will have to be built up and the people you need to approach will work in both large and small companies, as well as already experienced professional make-up, hair and costume people. As a beginner, it may be possible to visit such people to see how they work. Most freelances will be reluctant to recommend anyone unless they are sure of their work. There are agencies that will act as an answering service for a fee, or will find you work if they are confident of your competence.
- **Business skills:** it helps to have an accountant, especially if you have to register for VAT. It is vital to keep your books in order as you go along, especially recording the replacement of small items. If you think you can do it at the end of the year, beware! It will take you weeks of valuable time when you could be working and having fun! Self-employment stamps must also be bought regularly or contributions can be paid automatically by setting up a direct debit to the Inland Revenue NI contributions office.

Working as freelance

Teamwork

Perhaps the most important quality needed to work successfully in this business is tolerance. Tolerance enables you to work alongside others as part of the team.

Many departments and personnel are needed to create a production, each needing time and support to do their job. Personalities will vary greatly, and each will have differing opinions. This, of course, adds to the excitement but can also cause some difficulties. There is enough tension created in this type of work without having to deal with personal disagreements. These have to be kept to a minimum.

Being part of a production team also means liaising with others. First the director will have ideas on how the make-up, hair and costume should look. Then the artist may have strong views. Along the way, others, for example the lighting director, may have problems that must be considered. Compromises and changes sometimes have to be made.

Each of us strives to do our work to the best of our ability, but this should not be at the expense of others. Sometimes we may have to accept something that could have been more successful for us personally but is, in all other respects, successful for others. Being understanding and flexible will be necessary. There may be a time when we need support and cooperation from colleagues in order to achieve what is really important to us. Developing the skills to relate to others in this way is important.

Members of the make-up and costume departments dry off artists after a rainy scene

Teamwork is most important in our own department. There may be a number of people with differing levels of skills and responsibilities. Although everyone will be busy doing her or his own work, it makes for a more successful department if each person is also aware of how help may be given to others. This may be holding grips and pins for someone creating a wonderful hairstyle, washing powder puffs ready for the next day, or simply making a cup of tea for someone who has not had a break.

On big productions, the ability to be part of a team will be a necessity. Work starts early in the morning and a 12-hour day is usually considered a short day. The people around you will be your friends and work colleagues constantly for the next few months. Breakfast, lunch and evening meals will be taken with your colleagues. Usually a close relationship develops and a great sense of loss is felt at the end of the production. Then, after a well-earned rest, with luck you will be on to your next assignment with a new group of people to get to know.

Teamwork

Working with others

Television and film production require many skills in many different departments, but it is necessary for all personnel to share knowledge of general production-making. Various departments have to work very closely together – cameras and sound, for instance, as it is necessary for them to negotiate moves together to prevent sound booms being in shot. Make-up, hair and costume naturally have to work closely, but they also need to understand lighting and can often enlist the help of the lighting director or camera operator. It is the knowledge and understanding of the various requirements and needs of each department that will create a helpful and professional production team.

The skills that members of all departments share are:

- the ability to work under pressure and to a tight schedule. No matter how prepared each member of the team thinks he or she is, each is affected by the whole team. A problem in one department may have a knock-on effect on others. You should be able to function individually, anticipating and concentrating, and yet be flexible and work as part of a coordinated team;
- having an attitude that enables you to be part of a team. Each of us strives to do our work to the best of our ability, but this should not be at the expense of others;
- resourcefulness and self-motivation. Being patient and tactful under stressful conditions, yet showing enthusiasm for even the most routine work;
- the ability to think quickly and objectively. Confidence comes with experience, but the object is to furnish the needs of the production and not be overwhelmed by feelings of anxiety or needs of your own;
- creative skills. Having sufficient training and understanding of the subject;
- listening skills. Having the ability to relate to others, particularly artists, and not overreacting under pressure.

Shooting on location often means working in confined spaces with each department wanting to see what is taking place. Sometimes it is just not possible for everyone to be on the set. If this is the case the assistant director will always call for final checks before any shot.

Only two artists on set but work needed by many staff

Conduct

It is important that standards of behaviour beneficial to the production are maintained.

Timekeeping

Every second counts in the making of programmes, especially for live television. Every member of the cast and crew is responsible for good timekeeping. One member being a few minutes late can affect the whole crew. This is especially important for make-up, hair and costume departments as they often start work before other departments. If a make-up, hair or costume call is 6.30 am, several people will be involved in seeing that the artist is there on time. It is the greatest sin, therefore, for the make-up, hair or costume person then to be late. People are not always at their best at that hour of the morning and it is important that adequate time be allowed to set up for work and to prepare a relaxed atmosphere.

Appropriate friendliness

A friendly crew is important to relieve the stress of production-making, but learning to judge the mood or the appropriateness of chat is important. Crew members may need to concentrate, and artists in particular may be getting into the 'mood' of their character or going over their lines. It is important that this is respected.

Attentiveness during rehearsals, transmission or recording

It is important to be aware that artists can be easily distracted by people talking and moving, or even just standing in their eye line. It is necessary to be sensitive to any behaviour that may distract others.

Transmission lights

Never enter a studio when the transmission lights are showing red or amber, which means a programme is in transmission or recording. When a blue light is showing, it is safe to go in.

Appropriate dress and behaviour in front of an audience

It is usual to wear clothes suitable for studio work in general without bringing attention to yourself. However, there are times, such as church services, concerts and celebrity awards, where formal dress will be required. Make-up, hair and costume personnel will need to take advantage of breaks in a recording to check artists, e.g. to powder noses or comb hair. If there is an audience present, this may invite comments from the 'warm-up artist' – someone who talks or jokes with the audience to keep them entertained. This is usually done in good humour and is of interest to the audience. Whereas this should not distress you, it is important not to join in with the fun! You are doing your job as quickly and efficiently as possible without becoming part of the entertainment.

Conduct

Safety

As with employment everywhere, safety for you and others is paramount. There are strict safety precautions and rules that apply in any studio; for example, no smoking, no consumption of food or drink in the studio.

The obvious personal safety requirement for make-up, hair and costume personnel is to wear appropriate clothing. You need to be ready to work in any conditions: in confined spaces, amongst scenery or in inclement weather. Ease of movement is indispensable. When working under pressure, the last thing you need to worry about is your clothing. Suitable footwear is not only important for comfort, as you will be spending many hours on your feet, but it is a regulation in studios that sensible soft-soled shoes be worn. Although moving around while recording is taking place should be kept to a minimum, it will sometimes be necessary to do so and without making any noise. You will also have to negotiate scenery, possibly in darkness, and to step over many cables that, although covered with ramps, will need careful attention.

Safety in the workroom is vital.

- There are now strict regulations to adhere to. Often all products kept in a department are tested by the Health and Safety department and will have a list of their contents recorded. If possible, it is advisable that all freelance staff do the same for their products; it may be that safety forms will need to be signed when employed on a production.
- It is important to know government regulations on the storage and use of potentially dangerous chemicals and these can be obtained at local Health and Safety offices. Cleaning fluids, either for clothes or for wigs, must be to Health and Safety standards and must be used in the appropriate manner and conditions.
- Bottles and products must be labelled clearly.
- Electrical equipment must be regularly checked and cleaned.
- Any materials used on another person, such as make-up foundations or skin products, should be safe to use and any possible allergic reaction checked for. If there are any doubts, allergy tests should be carried out.
- Equipment used on a person's skin or hair must be cleaned and sterilized before being used again.
- Wraps and towels, and any clothing supplied, should be laundered.
- There must be adequate personal liability insurance. Employers will ensure staff are covered, but freelance workers must *always* have their own insurance cover.

You have a responsibility to ensure satisfactory safety standards, otherwise you may lose compensation for any injury or illness you sustain and may even be prosecuted for injury or illness you cause to others. Ask the production manager if you are not sure of anything and report all accidents, however small.

Multi-skilling

This is still a very difficult area to consider. On one level, having a wide-ranging knowledge of techniques and production skills is necessary, flexibility being an important attribute. On another level, having such capabilities can result in problems and it is important to understand why.

At one time it was possible, financially, to employ sufficient staff for all departments and each person had a specific job. However, that has changed and accountants govern the world! Sometimes, for a production to be made at all, multi-skilling has to be considered. Multi-skilling should be dictated only by the script requirements, which in turn affect the schedule and facilities.

There are sometimes very practical reasons for some departments to combine skills, e.g. make-up and hairdressing:

- time can be saved if one person can work with one artist on both make-up and hair;
- the artist may feel more comfortable with the same person looking after all aspects;
- one person can then design the whole illusion and keep continuity notes for each artist.

Because of financial constraints, it is now sometimes necessary for one person to be asked to do make-up, hair and wardrobe. If this is all within the expertise of that person, this flexibility could be offered. However, the production team and the artist concerned should be aware of the difficulties that may be caused by such an arrangement. A make-up artist cannot attend to a problem on the studio floor if she or he is ironing a shirt for another artist. This is not necessarily understood. Someone caught up in this situation must be careful not to compromise her or his own position. It may be possible, however, to have a 'runner' or work-experience person to help as an extra pair of hands.

Working in this way has its problems but it sometimes has to be considered if the alternative is to lose the production or to employ no make-up or wardrobe personnel and make poor quality pictures.

Studios

Although studios vary in size, they are similar in all other ways. The main studio must have certain necessities such as soundproofing, special floor surfaces that can be painted and rigging facilities for lighting. There will be a workforce permanently employed at the studio to maintain it and to prepare it for each production. Sometimes this will require overnight working to ready the studio for the next day.

Around the studio are all the technical galleries and other rooms required for production. In a small studio there may be only one make-up and dressing room but large studios will have separate facilities for make-up and costume, as well as facilities for the art department such as a props department, greenrooms or hospitality rooms, and dressing rooms for the artists. Some large studios will have their own camera and lighting equipment; those that don't will have to have the space for such equipment to be brought in.

The technical galleries, or control rooms, will include one for the production team to work in, one for the lighting department and one for the sound department. Here there will be monitors to see the pictures from the various cameras and the technical desks necessary to produce good pictures and sound. There are monitors in the studio itself, but those in the production gallery or the lighting gallery are more accurately balanced. Make-up, hair and costume staff may need to check their work there. There is limited space in a control gallery so entry should be kept to a minimum. It is necessary to be quiet and to show respect for others working.

A working studio

Facilities for make-up, hair and costume will vary according to the size of the studio. At one time, all television studios had their own staff and their own materials and equipment. Nowadays, very few do and materials and equipment have to be provided by staff working on the production or by the production itself. Most studios will have a make-up room or dressing room with a large mirror surrounded by working lights. There should be no daylight coming into a studio make-up room, as the lighting should be sympathetic to studio lighting.

There are, of course, very strict rules of conduct while working in studios and only authorized personnel are admitted. Every studio will have warning lights above the entrance door. When rehearsal is taking place a blue light will show, but when recording is taking place the light will be red, signalling no entry at any cost. No food or drink should be taken into a studio.

Appropriate dress and behaviour is necessary in a studio. There are many cables and much technical equipment to be avoided, and camera and sound personnel have to have freedom of movement. They will be concentrating on their work and it is essential for other staff to be aware of this and not to get in the way.

Production staff

Several departments will work to create the final production but, when working in a studio, certain of them will not often meet up. This is unlike location work, for example in film production, where it is possible to see most departments working alongside each other.

First there is the production team. This includes the producer, director, production manager, production assistant, and floor manager and assistants. Apart from the floor manager and assistants, who join the team once back in the studio, the production team will have been working together for some time, each person joining the team when appropriate. The producer and director will have set up the production, possibly finding the financial backing, organizing scriptwriters and casting the artists. The production manager then joins the team to organize the staff and the facilities required. If location work is involved, a location manager is needed early in the production planning to find suitable locations.

Production team

- *Producer:* in television, the producer may not necessarily have the responsibility of financing the production. He or she is much more involved with the making or the 'look' of the production.
- *Director:* plans the production artistically and directs all aspects of it.
- *Production assistant:* works with the director in the preparation of the production, is responsible for timing and calling the shot numbers when transmitting or recording.
- *Floor manager:* directs the work on the studio floor. He or she has talkback to the production control gallery and coordinates the two.
- *Floor assistant:* organizes the requirements on the studio floor, such as calling the artists when they are needed.

Make-up, hair and costume are part of the design section, along with the lighting and art departments. On a large production each head of department will join the team several weeks before starting production to plan their individual undertakings. Production meetings then take place where the heads of departments meet to discuss the script requirements and the staff needed.

Once in the studio, other members of each department join the production: for example make-up artists, hairdressers and costume dressers. Other studio floor personnel, such as scene-hands and electricians, technical operations staff (including the camera department and sound), other members of the design teams and the art department also come on board. There may also be a prompter operator who controls the script text that is displayed on a screen attached to the front of the camera for the presenter to read.

There may be a final post-production stage, where the material is edited and audio dubbed. Any graphics are added at this stage.

Changes are discussed by production staff

Once recording starts only the appropriate staff will be working 'on set', especially if recording is taking place in a confined space.

As a studio is designed to allow different departments to have their separate areas, it does mean that some departments may never meet up.

Rehearsal

Some drama and situation comedies need extensive rehearsal time, which will begin with a 'read through'. This is the first time all artists, production staff and heads of departments meet together to read through the script. Rehearsals then continue over several weeks in halls or rehearsal rooms with the director, production assistant, floor manager and artists. This is a good opportunity for designers to meet artists and discuss problems. On other productions, especially news bulletins, rehearsal will be a brief read through a short time before transmission.

No production can be transmitted without any rehearsal. Not only do artists and presenters need rehearsal time, but also technical operations must be put into place. Cameras have to be set up, lighting must be checked and sound equipment needs to be tested. Camera shots and lighting will have been planned, in principle, in pre-production time, but once in the studio adjustments have to be made.

Rehearsal time is important for all departments and, though sometimes it seems as though 'nothing is going on' and time is being wasted, somewhere something is being done!

Live productions

If a production is being transmitted 'live', sufficient time has to be allowed for rehearsal of the whole before it is transmitted without breaks. News bulletins are transmitted in this manner daily, often with a remotely controlled camera in the studio. Concerts, operas and similar 'live' entertainment need a great deal more planning and rehearsal, certainly a whole day and sometimes several days for one evening's transmission.

Rehearse/record

Pre-recording on tape or film means that sections of the work can be rehearsed and then immediately recorded, resulting in a much higher quality of work. Mistakes can be corrected and changes in scenery, costume and make-up can be made. It also means that a production can be filmed out of sequence. There are many reasons for doing this, not only financial. The availability of locations is a main consideration. It may be that part of the production requires an artist to be soaked with water, so for continuity reasons all the 'dry' scenes would need to be recorded consecutively.

Working in this way means that a production can be planned in advance in great detail and rehearsal time gives the various departments an opportunity to see the results of their planning and to make improvements.

There is generally a system of rehearsing once in the studio:

■ *blocking:* this is looking at shots with or without artists, giving every department a chance to see what is needed;

- *a run-through:* this is a rehearsal with artists and includes any inserts or changes, giving an indication of the timing of the shots and the camera moves etc.;
- *a dress run-through:* this is a full rehearsal, from titles to credits, showing requirements of the whole production.

Rehearsal time is also used by make-up, hair and costume personnel to do other work, such as preparing for another scene or even another day.

The camera waits while artists rehearse

Transmission: live and recorded

To limit the dangers posed by noise and distractions only key personnel are allowed in the studio while transmission takes place. Nobody should enter the studio once transmission begins. The red light outside the studio door will flash to inform people that transmission is taking place. All staff should be in the studio ready for last minute checks in plenty of time. The floor manager will give a countdown to the start of transmission, the set will be cleared of unnecessary staff and silence will be required as the last thirty seconds are counted. If staff do have to move around in the studio, great care must be taken for safety reasons, and to avoid obstructing the camera and sound department or getting in the eyeline of artists.

If the production is 'live', there will be no chance to make any adjustments once transmission begins and any mistakes will go out 'on air'! For the design departments this also means that quick changes will be limited, as they can only be made off-camera, i.e. when an artist is not in the scene being transmitted or when a set is not being used. It may be that there is a section of film or pre-recording that is inserted into the programme. That will be very precisely timed and may give opportunities for checks or changes. The floor manager will then be responsible for clearing the set of unwanted staff and counting the studio back on air.

In a rehearse/record situation, the tension is a little less as only short sections are recorded at a time. This allows for greater freedom for design teams to

The studio prepares for transmission

36

work, and changes in make-up, hair and costume can be planned to take place in breaks.

Although make-up, hair and costume departments have to do the bulk of their work at the beginning of the day, some make-up calls have to be during rehearsal time. Artists appearing in the first scene are obviously given the earliest calls, and throughout the day artists required for other scenes are called appropriately.

There are usually monitors in the studio for personnel to see the pictures being transmitted, but these will not necessarily be so well tuned as those in the lighting gallery. This is where a make-up or costume designer will need to be to see accurate pictures.

Transmission: live and recorded

Standing by on set

There should be someone from each department standing by on set. Sometimes this may only need to be one person. If it is a large production, the make-up, hair and costume staff usually have certain artists to look after, and it is not uncommon for everyone to be on set. This is mainly for continuity reasons, especially for films, when each scene is broken down into a series of sequences. It is important to know whether the coat was open or closed, or whether the hair was behind the ears or not. For the make-up department, a constant watch has to be kept for shiny faces as the lights and rooms get increasingly hot.

To save time during filming it will be necessary for each department to have a box on set that contains tools and small amounts of anything that may be useful. As well as a general set box, a make-up artist may keep a separate bag for each artist, keeping their brushes and make-up, especially lipstick colours, always at hand. Something you will always see a make-up artist with is cologne! When a cologne-soaked cloth is shaken, the movement causes the cologne to evaporate and the cloth feels extremely cold. This is ideal for cooling artists. Chamois leathers are popular for this but, as a different cloth is needed for each artist for hygienic reasons, velour powder puffs are just as good.

When watching continuity it is necessary to be aware of the type of shot being made:

- for a 'long shot' there is no need to worry about close details that are unlikely to be seen;
- for a 'medium shot' there may be two or more artists in view and only obvious continuity areas need to be checked, such as clothing and hair;
- in a 'close up', small details such as shine and lipstick are important.

Before each scene, or shot in the case of location work, the floor manager or first assistant will call for make-up and costume checks. Learn to see what is really necessary: there is nothing more irritating for artists or for the director than staff fussing over things that would not be noticed.

Make-up and wardrobe facilities

All television studios will have make-up and wardrobe facilities, although the smaller studios may just have dressing rooms with make-up mirrors. In this case the make-up artist or hairstylist will have to carry all equipment with them, packing up after each make-up. The artists' clothes would be left in their dressing rooms and the wardrobe person would arrange a suitable time to call to see if all is well. It is likely that another room would have to be made available for the wardrobe personnel for any ironing or storing of extra clothes.

The larger studios will have a separate make-up room where the make-up artists can base themselves, setting out their equipment ready for each artist to come to them at a given time. Some larger studios also have limited stock and electrical equipment available.

Dressing rooms do generally have washing facilities, a toilet and shower. Make-up rooms usually have washing facilities; if not, water must be readily to hand. Make-up rooms have large mirrors with either single light bulbs around them or fluorescent tubes. These lights are to eliminate unnatural shadows so that the make-up can be well balanced. They will also show the effect of studio lighting.

The larger studios are likely to have good facilities for the costume department. There will be a large wardrobe area with plenty of hanging space for clothes, large tables for sorting through accessories or for dressmaking. The dressmaking area may be separate and there will be a laundry area where clothes can be washed and ironed.

A make-up room with three or more work spaces

Location work

Any work away from what is considered the production's base is categorized as location work. Extra time and expense should be considered and allowed for staff travelling. However, freelance personnel consider their home as base, and so this would not necessarily apply; they would simply be told where the location is. Either way, extra time has to be allowed to find the location and to set up and prepare for work before artists arrive. The make-up, hair and costume personnel may be the first at the location and may have to find their own way to whatever facilities are available. This is when location work can be at its most frustrating. If the recording is at somebody's house there may not be adequate facilities laid on. A bedroom may be used for both make-up and costume. There may not be enough space or a table for equipment or adequate lighting. Electric plugs are always in the wrong place! More frustrating still, of course, is filming in a remote spot in the countryside with no electricity, water or toilets available. This is when your calm, tolerant personality will be tested and the need to adapt and take things in your stride will be paramount.

In view of the extra travelling, it is likely that the working hours will be longer. On a larger production the first person on site will be the location manager. He or she will have planned the day's work and who needs to be where and when. Next to arrive will be make-up, hair and wardrobe personnel, probably long before the rest of the production team. At the end of the day, when everyone else is going home, make-up, hair and wardrobe staff will still be cleaning off make-up, collecting wigs, washing and ironing and generally preparing for the next day's work.

Location work differs from studio work in that members of different departments are thrown together more. They do not always have separate areas in which to carry out their work and so this is often a very good opportunity to learn how other departments work. However, consideration has to be given to the fact that although there may seem to be a lull in activity in one department, others are often working. It is also important to be aware that although make-up, hair and wardrobe may have temporarily finished their work and have time on their hands, standing around chatting can be annoying and does not look very professional. Generally these times are good opportunities to clear up and prepare for later.

It is sensible to think ahead, too, not only for work purposes but for breaks. Any official breaks may be a busy time for make-up, hair and costume departments, and it may be that staff of these departments need to take a break when they can. Cover can be offered by other members of the team.

If the location work is out of doors, more accurate continuity notes are required. If the scene is not linked to any interior shots and is completed in one day there is less to worry about. If it is linked to indoor shots, e.g. the artist returns home from an outing, which may be shot several days or weeks later, accurate notes of the hair and clothes will be necessary. The weather will have an impact on how, or even whether any work is done at all that day! Obviously,

Location work provides an opportunity to see different departments working in close proximity on set

if at all possible, rather than lose the whole day the location will be changed, therefore the schedule may also be changed. This may mean different artists altogether and will not only depend on whether the artists are available but also on whether the costume and make-up requirements can be met.

Ultimately, the work has to be done come rain or shine and it may be that compromises have to be made by all. Very often location work can be extremely frustrating, not having the right facilities or trying to keep an artist looking presentable in a gale force 9! Tolerance, patience and understanding are all necessary qualities for this kind of work. If you have these, location work is fun. It is challenging, healthier than working in a studio, friendlier as you work in closer union with other departments and, at the end of the day, if it is horrible, you know it will end and you need never go there again!

Preparation for location work

The preparation necessary for location work depends on the commission. At the simplest level you may only be given the location. You may not know the name of the artist or what is needed. In this situation you require a kit that is comprehensive enough to provide for all occasions, a route plan and sufficient time to get there.

If the assignment is to join an ongoing production, perhaps to work for a few days with 'extras' – actors employed as background artists – there will be a make-up, hair or wardrobe designer to give you instructions. If there is anything specific needed, such as facial hair or wigs, this will be provided for you. It will be expected that cleaning and preparation for another time will be done at the end of the day even if your particular work is finished earlier.

If you are a designer on a production, then there is a great deal more preparation needed. If the production is very large, you would have had a script, have planned what is needed, agreed a budget and attended planning meetings with other heads of department. It will be your responsibility to provide everything required for your department. This may mean packing a lot of equipment and arranging for it to go to the location. Any designer knows to be ready for the unexpected. Even for small productions, many bags will need to be packed. If other staff are joining you, it is your responsibility to see that they have somewhere to work and that they are given contracts and times.

Sometimes it is impossible to go back to base if you have forgotten something!

Outside broadcasts

Outside broadcasts are for events that cannot be provided from the studio. They are either transmitted live or recorded as if live. The 'studio' goes out to these events in the form of large vans full of technical equipment and galleries. Cables are run from the vans to the cameras and sound equipment. The production team sits in the broadcasting vans just as they would do in a studio. They are able to see the pictures being produced and to adjust and change them as necessary.

Sporting events are covered in this way and generally make-up, hair and wardrobe staff are not needed. However, concerts and theatre productions can entail a great deal of work for such personnel.

As the location of the van and the complex cable system is important, there will be a location manager in charge of operations. If the production is from a theatre or opera house, there will be make-up, hair and wardrobe facilities within the building. It would be like working on location. Just as they do in the studio, by watching the monitors in the outside broadcast van during rehearsals make-up, hair and wardrobe personnel can see their work. This gives an opportunity to make any necessary adjustments.

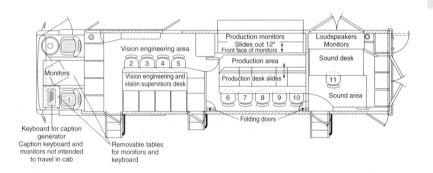

Layout – outside broadcast control room

1 Caption generator operator
2 Vision engineer
3 Vision supervisor
4 Vision engineer
5 Vision engineer
6 Engineering manager

7 Editor/producer
8 Vision mixer
9 Director
10 Production assistant
11 Sound supervisor

An outside broadcast van showing technical areas (*Source: TV Technical Operations: An Introduction*, Peter Ward, Focal Press 2000)

Location personnel

The production staff and the design teams required for location work are the same as those for television work. Additional staff needed for film work are:

- *Financier:* someone who commissions and/or finances the production;
- *Accountant:* responsible for the everyday financial requirements, such as expenses and salaries;
- *Production Manager:* responsible for budget and schedules: weekly schedules and daily schedules which are then distributed to all production staff;
- *Coordinator:* coordinates and liaises between location staff and the production office;
- *First Assistant Director:* in charge of the smooth running of location filming;
- *Second Assistant Director:* coordinates and organizes the requirements for each day's shooting. It is usually the Second Assistant Director who liaises with heads of make-up, hair and costume departments about calls for the artists;
- *Third Assistant Director:* assists the First Assistant Director on location;
- *Script Supervisor:* watches continuity between shots and scenes.

On feature films there are many other departments and personnel involved:

- a casting director is required to recommend and audition artists, working alongside the producer or director;
- a unit nurse will be on hand at all times and, if there are animals, a vet will also be required;
- camera departments will be larger, e.g. they will include a much larger grips department – people experienced in setting up tracking and other special camera requirements.

As films use more and more special effects the list of credits gets longer and longer! The pyrotechnics department will be separate from the stunt people and there may be a model-making department as well as a prosthetics department. There are then the post-production departments involved in special effects and digital work.

Setting up shots on a moving bicycle. The director looks on while the first assistant gives last-minute notes. The sound assistant and the camera operator are on board the trailer, while the costume assistant and make-up artist travel in the cab.

Location facilities

Depending on the production, facilities on location will vary. If the location is a house or larger building, then facilities such as water and toilets will exist and it will simply be a matter of arranging with the production assistant which rooms are available for you to use. You will need to make sure that there is adequate light and sufficient chairs and tables for your use. It will not be as convenient as working in a studio.

If you are involved in filming for a larger production, then the location manager will have organized all facilities from toilets to catering services. There may be make-up, hair and wardrobe vans available; hopefully you will have been consulted beforehand to ensure they are adequate. The vans will vary in size, but will be specially designed for make-up, hair and wardrobe. They will have the necessary lighting and furniture and there will be water and heating on board. Occasionally there are small vans that cater for both departments, but usually they are separate. This is preferable, as having people moving around when a make-up artist is working is not good. The vans have to be very stable.

It is important to make sure your workplace is close to the filming, as you need to be on hand at all times during shooting.

Sometimes an artist will have a personal motor home as a dressing room, and it may be necessary to work in there.

Catering vans and dining buses are provided. Sometimes make-up, hair and wardrobe staff prefer to take their food to their own vans. Occasionally they have

Workspace inside a caravan is very cramped and staff need to be extremely organized

to make special arrangements to eat earlier than others to leave time to check their work before filming starts again. It is very rare that make-up, hair and wardrobe staff have their full hour's meal break. Sometimes there is no break at all!

Care has to be taken not to forget to check when an artist is finished!

A cup of tea 'on the run'

Understanding light and colour

Light travels in waves. The eye is able to perceive colour because each colour has a wave of different lengths. Reds have the longest wavelengths and blues the shortest. When light is passed through a glass prism its waves split according to their length and can be 'seen' as separate colours – red, orange, yellow, green, blue, indigo and violet – always in that order, the order of the rainbow. The human eye is able to perceive certain light wavelengths which enable us to see these colours.

Light is absorbed or reflected by surfaces. If most of the light is reflected, we 'see' white; if most is absorbed, we 'see' black. The colour we perceive depends on how much light is reflected and how much is absorbed by the surface.

We can make coloured products by taking the primary colours, red, blue and yellow, and mixing them together in a variety of ratios to produce secondary colours – oranges, greens and violets. The colour wheel illustrates how colours can be mixed.

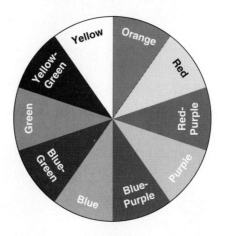

Artists' colour wheel

The colours opposite each other on the wheel are known as complementary colours. When put next to each other they can produce a striking effect. All three primary colours mixed together will produce grey. This can also happen when too many colours are mixed together.

- *Brightness* – is the intensity of a colour, how dark or light it is.
- *Hue* – is the term used for the separate colours: red, blue, green, etc.
- *Tone* – is created by mixing colours; it can range from almost pure colour or hue to grey.
- *Tint* – is made by mixing white with a colour.
- *Shade* – is made by mixing black with a colour.

The colours of artificial lighting do not respond to mixing in the same way as paint colours. The primary lighting colours are red, green and blue. Combined equally, they produce 'white' light. When a colour filter is used, only the wavelengths matching the filter's colour will pass through it, all other wavelengths are absorbed. This enables the lighting technician to vary the light effects by using different shades and tints of gelatins or colour filters.

Using gelatin (often known as 'gel') over a light will, of course, affect the colours of everything it shines on. Shining red light on a red paint colour will wash out the colour, theoretically to white, while using a green light on the red paint will make it appear almost black. Both skin tones and costume colours will be affected by coloured gels.

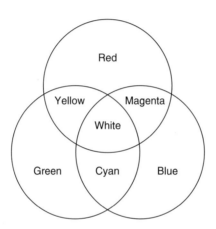

Lighting colour wheel

Lighting

The most basic requirement for lighting is to provide sufficient light to expose the pictures in the camera, but lighting can also influence shape, depth, the character of the scene, atmosphere, composition and can direct the eye to a particular part of the scene. Skilful use of light on a face can accentuate or minimize the good or the bad features of the person being photographed.

It is essential that lighting and make-up work closely together. A lighting director will take into consideration all the shadows his or her lights will produce and aspects such as reflections in spectacles and contact lenses, while the make-up department corrects the smaller imperfections.

The overall aim of any production, whether it be TV, film or photography, is to achieve pictures that are sympathetic to the subject and comfortable to look at. The public may not be aware that they are looking at good pictures, but they would most certainly be distracted by bad pictures. For example, if an artist is wearing no make-up, has a heavy beard line and the jacket he is wearing is strobing, by the time the viewer has thought how awful he looks they have missed what was being said!

A lighting director will take into consideration:

- a wide variety of lighting units that can be broadly considered in two groups – those giving *hard* light (that is, producing hard shadows) and those giving *soft* light (that is, producing soft shadows). Often both types of unit are used on the same scene. The most important factors are the placement of the lights, their angle and position relative to the camera and artist, and the balancing of the different intensities;
- key lights. These are strong directional lights giving modelling and structure to a shot. The mood of the picture will be determined by how much light they produce – high key or low key;
- fill lights. These are a softer source of light often placed on the opposite side to the key light. They can be moved around easily and may have flaps on each side, called 'barn doors', which can be closed or opened to narrow or widen the effects. Coloured gels can be clipped to these lights to create different effects;
- backlight. Sometimes a feeling of space between the artist and the background is required, and a light directed behind the subject will highlight the head;
- background light. To give sufficient light to the background without overpowering the foreground.

Lighting a face or a whole person

Fill lights are extremely important when lighting faces. Too much top lighting will create harsh shadows around the eyes and nose. A heavy fringe or long hair falling forward can shade the face. Only a certain level of correction can be made by a make-up artist; help will be needed by adding a fill light. However, the level of light is critical: too much light creates flat, dead pictures and too much light on a foreground subject can 'burn it out', that is, colour is bleached out and the face looks as though it has a high shine on it.

It is important for make-up, hair and costume staff to understand the principles of lighting so that they can recognize if there is anything they can do to enhance the picture or whether they need to discuss what is to be done with the lighting director. Generally lighting directors are extremely helpful when make-up alone will not suffice.

When a whole scene is being shot, the lighting has to be more general and cannot focus primarily on one subject. When lighting a person, as in an interview or a news bulletin, then the lighting can be much more specific.

Make-up
Top lighting will create shadows underneath any bone structure. Particularly difficult shadow areas are:

- under the eyebrows;
- bags or lines under the eyes;
- nose to mouth lines;
- hollow cheeks;
- under the chin.

Top lighting will also highlight the top of the head but cause heavy shadows under fringes and at the side of the face and neck if the artist has long hair.

Costume
As well as being aware of the colours in an artist's costume, the following points should be considered:

- white is not used often as it is difficult for lighting;
- red also has the effect of 'bleeding' around the edges so is best avoided;
- stripes and small patterns close together can create a strobe effect;
- the contrast between skin tone and costume must be considered – black skin and pale yellow would be a challenge for lighting;
- shiny fabrics may also cause difficulties for lighting, just as coloured gels may affect the colour of costumes.

Studio lighting

In the studio there is a vast, permanent rigging system in the ceiling, numbered and mapped out so that a lighting director and even a sound supervisor can plan in advance where their main lights and microphones will be for a scene. These can all be put in place in advance of a production and can be turned on and off when needed. They are operated from a gallery where colour and temperature can be checked out by any other design personnel.

On the studio floor will be any other necessary lighting, the heavy cables covered by bridges for the safety of people moving around the studio. Once lights are set it is important that they are not knocked and that people take care not to walk in front of them when in use.

Lights are set for the studio requirements

If the studio has a make-up room, the lights around the mirrors should be compatible with the lighting in the studio. Different bulbs, especially fluorescent bulbs, have different colour temperatures. If the bulbs are too orange, they will affect the make-up colours chosen, which will then not look right when in the studio. Some fluorescent tubes have cooler colours resembling daylight. Unfortunately not all dressing rooms have good lighting, and this will be noticeable while working. Inadequate lighting will affect the work you do and all make-up must be checked on a well-balanced monitor.

Location lighting

Obviously, the lighting used on location depends not only on the production but also on the location. Outside broadcasts from an opera house or a theatre will entail more heavy lighting and there will be a means of rigging the extra lights, as in a studio. Filming on location necessitates lights being moved and changed constantly. Filming entails a different way of working in that each scene is broken up into several sequences; these are filmed separately and then put together. This means that the lighting is crucial as all the sequences have to match. It may be that for filming out of doors minimal lighting will be used, but for each shot the lighting director has to measure the amount of light available with a light meter, to determine whether it matches the previous shot. Often a crew will be waiting patiently for the sun to come out again and, if it doesn't, extra lighting will have to be used.

It is especially important that make-up, hair and costume people check their work in daylight when working out of doors. The work will have been done indoors and it is unlikely that the lighting facilities will have been good enough to engender complete confidence. If ever in any doubt about anything, the camera operator may be able to advise or reassure. The camera operator may even consult the appropriate personnel themselves if they see something that does not look quite right.

Extra lights are sometimes needed to boost the low levels of daylight

Production control

In studios there are areas, or galleries, where the director and technical supervisors work. There are three galleries, sometimes called control rooms, necessary:

- lighting gallery;
- sound gallery;
- production control.

They may be together as one open-plan area or separated as three different galleries. Each gallery has a monitor for every camera operating on the studio floor so that pictures can be adjusted. It is from the largest gallery, production control, that the director decides which camera shot is to be shown at any given time.

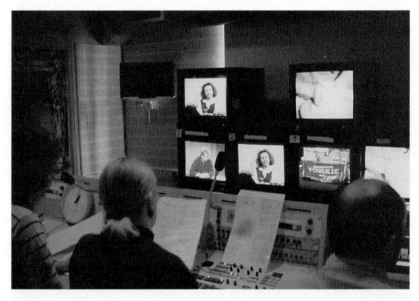

Production control gallery

Camera angles and shots are planned in advance. However, it is only when the whole studio is working and the shots are seen that decisions about any necessary changes can be made. The director talks to the camera operators through headphones and between them they work out what is needed. The camera operators work from a shot list clipped to their cameras and the production team work with a script, making the changes as they go along.

It is the production assistant, sitting next to the director, who calls out the shot numbers to the crew on the studio floor. She/he times the show and cues in any pre-recorded inserts when necessary.

On the other side of the director is the vision control desk and the vision mixer who is responsible for switching between cameras and other vision sources.

Also working from this gallery is the vision control operator responsible for the colour control and the setting up of the cameras. It is here that any technical adjustments are made, such as by using the chroma key (see 'Chroma key', in the section on Editing, page 58). A producer or editor may work from here overseeing the production and there may also be a caption-generator operator who adds captions to pictures.

In the lighting and vision control room, the lighting director and console operator work from the lighting plot, balancing the lights and making any changes and lighting effects.

The sound supervisor works in the sound control gallery. He or she talks directly to sound assistants on the studio floor. There may be an assistant who is responsible for adding music and sound effects.

It is to the production control gallery or the lighting gallery that the costume and make-up personnel can go to check their work. As in any gallery, entrance is restricted to necessary personnel. No talking is allowed and certainly no food or drink. Respect must be shown to the people working there.

Production control

Film cameras

Film cameras need to be much more portable than studio cameras. They are set up on tripods or various rigging equipment according to the type of shot required. Today a lot of camera work is hand held and there are specially designed cameras that balance themselves automatically for this type of work. For film production more camera personnel are needed in the department and the training requirements differ.

Rigging a camera may be a long and complicated process, sometimes requiring tracking to be laid down or cranes to be used for high shots showing a large area. Many things have to be taken into consideration, from setting up the shot to completion:

1. The placing of the camera is determined by whether it is to be a long shot or a close up.
2. The shot affects the type of rigging used. It may be a simple tripod or the camera may need to be placed on a 'dolly', a wheeled cart with a seat for the operator. Trained camera riggers set up the rigging.

A tripod

3. The camera is loaded with film or, if film is already in use, it is checked for quantity remaining by the camera assistant or 'loader'.
4. The lens is checked to see that it is clean. It is checked again at the end of each shot. If there is a 'hair in the gate', the shot will have to be repeated.
5. Rehearsals take place for the artists, cameras, lighting and sound. The focus is worked out and checked by the focus puller.

A dolly

6. Several 'takes' may be necessary before the director is happy with the outcome.
7. When the film is fully exposed it is put in a can, labelled and sent to be developed overnight to make sure all is well. The camera is re-loaded.
8. The developed shots are then returned to the director to check that he or she is happy. These are known as 'rushes', as the picture quality may not be as technically correct as the final film.

Small film productions rely mostly on one camera but sometimes, for major shots, a second camera will be used. If time is short, a second camera unit will be sent off to do other work for the production. This may or may not require make-up, hair and costume. Feature films may have several units working at the same time.

Unlike working in a studio where there are monitors, it is not easy for costume, hair and make-up personnel to see their work on camera. Although film cameras now use 'video assist', a video camera mounted alongside the camera to allow the director to monitor shots, the responsibility for the picture lies with the camera operator. He or she can see what is required and may need to liaise with other departments. If other departments have concerns, they need to check with the camera operator or the director of photography.

Editing

Just as the secret of good make-up is that it is not 'seen', the skills and techniques of an editor are invisible to the audience. As members of the public watch their favourite programme, they are unaware that it has been constructed from many different shots, possibly taken from many different angles. It seems like one continuous event. An editor selects and coordinates one shot with another to achieve a flow of images. The sound also has to be synchronized with the visual material. An editor plays a major part in the production, whether it is creating an atmosphere in a drama or constructing a news item.

Large studios have their own editing suites that are hired by each production when required. This is normally when production is completed. If, however, there is pre-filming that has to be shown to an audience, for example, the editing will have to be planned for in advance.

Film productions book an editing suite for the whole of a production as the rushes, i.e. the film that has been shot that day, need to be developed and very roughly put together each night. The rushes are then sent back for the director to see. It is sometimes possible also for heads of departments to see the rushes to check their own work. If all is well, the editors continue with their work and the major editing will then take place.

Chroma key

It is possible to superimpose one image onto another with the use of an electronic switch called a chroma key. This is operated from the vision mixing panel and requires the cameras, lighting and design set-up to be correct, as well as the make-up, hair and wardrobe. A background colour is chosen as a separation key, i.e. anything in that colour will be blanked out. Usually green is used, as blue is a popular colour for clothes, but other colours can be used. The subject to be in the foreground is placed in front of the large, flat coloured background, generally known as a 'flat', and shown on one camera while the required background is shown on another camera.

Camera 1

Camera 2

Chroma key switched on. Note that the hair must be carefully dressed.

The chroma key creates a kind of stencil of the subject by blacking out and isolating it. This 'stencil' can then be placed on the chosen background to enable the subject to be accurately placed. The cameras, of course, have to be locked off (i.e. made immovable or very steady) and a special viewfinder is used that shows both shots in one so that the pictures can be accurately

Placing the 'stencil' accurately

Adding the subject to the chosen background

aligned. The image has to fit perfectly as the keying switch can be confused easily, causing the foreground picture to break up around the edges.

This means that when the subject is an artist make-up, hair and costume personnel have an important part to play. Hair has to be carefully controlled so that hairs don't fly about causing the edges to break up. The colour that is used as the separation key cannot be used in the make-up or costume as this would blank out too! There is also a danger of colour from the background spilling over into the foreground. These factors mean that this is a slow and highly technical way of creating an illusion.

It is also possible to show an artist appearing behind an object by painting the object in the keying colour and placing this in front of the artist to create the 'stencil', which is then filled with the real image from the second camera.

As this is such a specialized way of working, it would be done separately in order not to interfere with the shooting of the rest of the production. However, costume, particularly, would have to be aware in advance in order to plan the choice of colours.

Requirements of different productions

Every production needs some preparation, but the costume and make-up aspects may require so little that the production assistant will be expected to organize them. The production assistant will have to tell artists when booking them that there will be no facilities for costume and make-up, that they must be prepared to bring a choice of costume and be responsible for how they look.

On small productions it may be that the make-up artist or costume assistant will not know who the artists are until arriving on location. That means that he/she has to be prepared for most situations. This entails carrying a lot of equipment and materials, especially make-up. Artists would bring clothes and colours that suit them, but the make-up artist has to be prepared for any skin or hair colour.

To be able to work as a make-up, hair or costume designer on larger productions it is necessary to understand the different requirements of productions, to be ready for any eventuality. These include:

- liaising with production staff and artists;
- script breakdown;
- budgeting;
- materials/product purchasing;
- continuity;
- wig/dress fittings;
- camera tests;
- quick changes;
- working with other departments;
- working with artists;
- responsibility for own staff.

Working with other departments

Preparation for a production will include liaising with other departments and artists. The director may have ideas about a character and so may the artist. However, there is a budget to consider and the designer, or head of department, will have to be aware of the needs of the whole production.

A production meeting is a chance for all departments to discuss their needs and to help each other if possible.

Even if there are no special requirements for an artist it is beneficial for the designer to contact them before the production begins. This will give the artist a chance to say if they have any worries about their make-up or clothes, and it encourages a good relationship and eases unnecessary anxieties.

Once the production is under way certain departments will work more closely together. Obviously, hair and make-up will need to work together and they will have to liaise with costume. Once on set, costume will work closely with the script supervisor, or continuity person.

There can also be a lot of hanging around, particularly on location when make-up, hair and costume have to be present and cannot get on with other jobs.

This is a good time to observe how other departments work, or simply to catch up with notes and paperwork.

Laying track and rigging cameras may take some time

Schedules

Planning for a large production includes dealing with a lot of paperwork. If not well organized it is easy to be overwhelmed by it.

1. Hopefully, the script will be the first document you have. This will have to be read before the production meeting or speaking to the director about requirements. There are times when the director will have to give an outline of what is required before the script is issued so that planning and research can go ahead.

2. After the production meeting has taken place, a running order or production schedule is issued. This is a plan of the order in which the scenes will be shot. A running order is a more simple document used mainly for studio productions, such as current affairs, educational programmes, quiz shows and situation comedies. It shows the order that the programme will take and often gives the running time of each item or scene. It will also show when any film or video is being inserted. A production schedule is usually a much more comprehensive document used on larger productions showing scenes and artists required over several weeks. It may also give important information, such as whether a particular scene is a day or night scene, whether the artists will get wet, or whether stunt artists are required. Naturally, when the filming gets under way and does not keep to schedule, it will have to be amended. The production schedule is a document which all departments need to work from.

3. Further into the planning, as the locations become finalized, a location schedule may be issued, giving greater details of locations.

4. During each day someone will finalize details for the following day's work. This may be the production assistant for studio work or the second assistant director on location. They will liaise with make-up, hair and costume staff about calls for the artists. At the end of the day a call sheet is issued. This gives the location (including a map), the scenes and artists required, the make-up and costume calls, and any other information regarding the next day's work. Sometimes it includes the expected weather!

From all these documents a designer or head of department will go on to plan for their own staff.

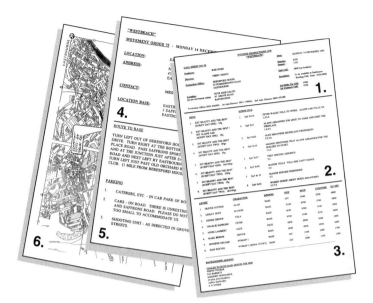

A location call sheet showing daily requirements

1. Production and production staff.
2. Description and numbers of scenes.
3. Artist and call times.
4. Location address and contacts.
5. Route.
6. Map.

Script breakdown

The first thing staff should receive is the script. Having read it, it is surprising how much more there is to be aware of or to plan for.

1. It is important to list all artists, extras and any other special requirements scene by scene. It may be that some artists never appear together and this will affect how many staff are required for the whole production. It is better for all if staff, make-up staff in particular, always look after the same artists. This is mainly for continuity purposes, but also for building up a good working relationship. Thus, it can be planned that one costume or make-up artist can look after a set number of artists in a given time.

   There are bound to be occasions when more artists appear in the same scene or on the same day than can be easily catered for. This requires the careful planning of call times for artists. Liaising with the first assistant director is important. Knowing the order of shooting of scenes facilitates efficient use of time.

2. A script breakdown then needs to be done for each character separately and any special requirements planned, such as make-up for ageing or illness. It will be necessary to plan this in advance in order to be ready for production meetings.

3. On a large production all departments may be involved in planning the production schedule – the order of shooting the scenes. This will be affected by the locations to be used and continuity issues such as artists having to get wet; it may be that all the 'dry' scenes have to be shot first. A finalized production schedule is then distributed to all staff to enable them to plan their own work.

4. Once shooting has started, the make-up, hair and costume call times for the next day have to be planned with the first assistant director or floor manager. A daily schedule, or call sheet, can then be issued with the scene numbers, the cast involved and the times they are required by each department. It is the designers' responsibility to give rough continuity notes to their staff, but it is the responsibility of the staff to then keep accurate day-to-day continuity notes.

Continuity

When productions were transmitted live there were few continuity problems as everything was shot in sequence. Once it was possible to rehearse and record, the problems of continuity grew. Recording provided so much more scope for the storyline and the timescale of the production. Even in a situation comedy, where the performance is in front of an audience in a studio, there can be location shots, filmed in advance and inserted into the studio recording. This means that the clothes worn and the make-up and hair presented, possibly weeks previously in the location work, must be matched exactly in the studio work.

Accurate notes must be kept and the use of a Polaroid or digital camera is extremely helpful. On a film unit a continuity person or production assistant takes photographs of every shot. Nowadays most departments have their own camera to enhance their own continuity notes.

The initial continuity can be planned in advance. The number of days covered by the story will be worked out first. Next, the time of day in each scene and how the time of each scene transposes into the following scene, which may even be set on another day, will be plotted.

Then, on the day shooting takes place, the actual work done, i.e. the clothes worn by the artists, their make-up and hairstyles, must be recorded in detail to be repeated for each applicable shot, which may be several days later. Obviously the production manager will try to minimize any continuity dilemmas, but there is always the serious possibility that a scene must be re-recorded at a later date.

Each designer will have their own method for recording notes, but it is paramount to have a system. There is always a possibility of the unexpected emergency when someone has to take over another's work. An intelligible and well-organized system will pay dividends. The details kept should contain:

- the artist's name;
- the name of the character portrayed;
- the episode, if applicable;
- the day involved, e.g., Day 1, Day 4, etc.;
- the detailed notes of work done or clothes worn. It is important for any hair ornaments used to be recorded and kept safe;
- any photographs taken can be stapled to these notes.

Obviously, if there are scenes when there is a major change for the artist, such as getting wet, dirty or being injured, the shooting schedule will have taken this into consideration in order to save time and, ultimately, money. The scene would probably be shot at the end of the day.

Budgeting

Generally the producer and the production manager will have decided upon a design budget as part of the production budget. The requirements of the designer are to work strictly within this budget. It is unlikely that the budget will be too high; no production manager is going to give money away! It is more likely that it will be too low, but it can be renegotiated if the designer has worked efficiently and can show the necessity of their requirements.

- Everyday materials will be needed, from foundations and hairspray to soap powders and cottons. These will vary depending on the number of artists involved, how many staff there are and how many days of shooting. Experience will enable a designer to judge how long materials last.
- Although every designer has their own kit, including electrical items, on a large production it may be necessary to buy more equipment, depending on how many extra staff are required.
- There are likely to be specific requirements for individual artists, whether for a wig and outfit for a character or a regular hair appointment for continuity purposes.
- On a large production spanning many months, it may be more cost-effective to purchase wigs and costumes than to hire them.
- The designer may have been contracted for a certain number of days' preparation, but if wig or dress fittings are required there may be extra days and expenses to be negotiated, both for the designer and the artist concerned. It is always as well to liaise with the production manager if in doubt.
- A costume designer will be familiar with artists liking the clothes so much that they want to buy them at the end of the production. This is obviously helpful in reducing costs, but should be regarded as a bonus rather than something to be counted on.

As the production progresses, all purchase orders with receipts attached are submitted to the production manager or accountant and their totals deducted from the overall budget. For large productions, money is drawn out as a float beforehand for smaller items; large invoices, for instance from costumiers and wigmakers, are given directly to the production manager.

Materials and product buying

The main concern for the design department is how the camera will react to the colours and fabrics being used. The human eye can only register a small range of the electromagnetic radio waves that enable radio and television transmissions. Although cameras today are very good, sometimes the tone of the colour will appear quite different on camera, or be unexpectedly affected by other colours present. A camera is more sensitive than the eye to red and will therefore accentuate any red in a colour that may not be clearly visible to the eye. For example, a foundation that appears to have a natural skin colour may look more orange on camera. This may be because it contains a high quantity of orange/red pigment or, for example, if a person is wearing a bright red shirt the red from the shirt may 'spill over' and affect the colour of the foundation.

The camera is also affected by very small designs in fabrics. A small stripe or dogtooth pattern of a suit, for instance, will cause the picture to strobe as the camera shot moves. Streaks of colour will break up the picture.

The first consideration, therefore, is to avoid using anything that the camera may not 'like'. There are suppliers who concentrate on making available colours that are suitable for TV and film. If in doubt, they are only too happy to give advice. It is likely that they have experience in the business.

If a department has permanent staff, stocktaking is a routine part of the job. There will be a system for checking and replenishing the materials and equipment regularly. Cleaning and checking electrical equipment would probably be done at the same time. For freelance staff, cleaning, restocking and checking the safety of their own equipment must also be done regularly.

For a designer working on a production, a major job will be planning, costing, and buying materials and equipment required for the production. She or he may need help with this task and may have an assistant to help. The bulk of the buying will be done before the production starts, but it will be necessary to replenish and buy items as it progresses.

Costume designers sometimes need to have clothes made by costume makers. The designers buy the fabrics and consult with the makers about their designs.

Camera tests

Camera tests are most commonly used for auditioning artists and TV presenters. For TV particularly, it is important for presenters to look good and to be heard clearly. Some of this they can learn, but the camera is unpredictable and some people are more photogenic than others. The same applies to sound: some people have a clearer speaking voice. Make-up, hair and costume personnel are not usually hired for these tests, unless many people are being tested and the production can afford it.

On a larger production, usually drama or feature films, there may be a special requirement for an artist and the director and the designer will want to make sure that everything looks right on camera. A special day will be organized for the artist and necessary personnel to attend. This will be in a studio and involve the lighting and camera personnel as well as some production staff.

This is a chance to see if clothes, make-up and hair are suitable and what changes may be needed. It obviously necessitates considerable expense so will happen only if really necessary. However, it is a good opportunity to learn and experiment. Being in a studio, the working conditions are good, as there are dressing rooms and mirrors. It is also an opportunity to get to know the artist and the character being portrayed. It may be the first time the various departments meet and it will set a precedent for all working together.

Quick changes

Sometimes there is a need for a very quick change of costume and make-up when shooting cannot stop for long, for example when transmitting a 'live' show or a situation comedy with an audience. Obviously this limits what can be done but, with the right kind of preparation, changes can be made.

All departments need to be alerted to the fact that a quick change will take place and it needs to be planned in advance:

- make-up, hair and costume personnel need to plan how the change is to take place. It may be that clothes are changed before any alterations to hair or make-up;
- it may be necessary to have help, e.g. one person holding equipment or clothes ready while another attends to the artist;
- where the quick change takes place is important to save crucial time. There may not be time to use the make-up room and an alternative room or space must be found and privacy provided. In studios it is easier to find a corner to set up a 'quick change room';
- the clothes and equipment or make-up needed must be previously set up and the staff ready and waiting for the artist concerned.

In the theatre some time can be saved by 'under dressing' or garments being constructed to be removed speedily.

It could be that every second counts and the quick change should be rehearsed to make sure that it is possible.

Wig and dress fittings

Wig fittings

If a wig is necessary, discussions will have taken place between the make-up artist or hairdresser and the director, if only to check the budget. Unless the company has its own wig department, e.g. as opera houses do, an appointment will be made with a wig supplier. If possible the make-up or hair designer attends the fitting with the artist to discuss the colour and the dressing of the wig. If that is not possible discussions have to be conducted on the telephone. However, once the artist is at the fitting, they will also have ideas and preferences. It is important that the artist feels happy, and compromises may have to be made by all.

The staff of the wig supplier know the stock well and will take accurate measurements of the head. If necessary they will know how to make any changes to the wig to make it suitable. Once a wig is chosen it is then sent to their dressing department where it is dressed into an appropriate style. The wig will be hired for the period of use and will be dispatched to the location when needed. It is the designer's responsibility to return the wig when it is no longer needed so that further hire charges are not incurred.

If it is not possible for an artist to attend a wig fitting, for instance if they are filming and cannot get away, it is possible to take an impression or measurements of their head to send to the suppliers (see page 144 for details).

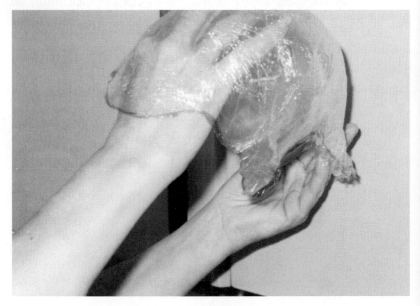

An accurately measured impression of an artist's head and hairline ready to send to the wigmakers

Dress fittings

Sometimes a costume designer is able to meet an artist to shop for particular clothes. This may be because the character requires a certain 'look' or it may just be to give advice and help in choosing clothes within the budget.

For some productions, particularly period productions, it may be necessary to hire costumes from a costumier. The designer will meet the artist at the costumier where there will be a large stock of costumes and a number of personnel on hand to measure and advise.

Designers also need to know costume makers who work as out-workers. This enables them to design specific costumes, buy the right kind of fabric and commission the work to be done. The costume maker usually meets the artist and the designer to take measurements, look at any pictures and discuss designs.

A costume being created

Productions and personnel

TV and film
There are many different types of production each with different personnel requirements. Budgeting and the quantity of work will affect the number of make-up staff required.

- *News items and bulletins.* A news and current affairs department often has a permanent staff, if just one or two people, depending on the hours of transmission. They are likely to have to employ freelance personnel for programmes above their normal output, such as during elections.
- *Documentaries.* These programmes don't usually require or use make-up or costumes unless they are period documentaries or reconstructions of events. Financial resources are usually limited.
- *Sporting events.* There are some sporting events that do require a make-up artist: snooker, for instance, where the sportspeople are seen in close-up.
- *Quiz shows.* A series will usually be recorded together. For example, if there are six shows they may be recorded two shows a day for three days. More than one make-up artist is usually required as often the competitors have to be kept apart.
- *Situation comedies.* These are productions that require a make-up designer who will join the production at the rehearsal stage to prepare for production. The required number of make-up staff will join when recording starts. These personnel will stay with the production all the way through, though freelance staff may be required for days when there are guest appearances or background artists.
- *Drama productions.* Apart from needing a make-up designer as above, the staffing for drama productions depends on the type of programme and the size of the cast. It could be a modern drama needing just two make-up personnel, or it may be period drama needing many staff, plus freelance personnel on quite a regular basis.

Feature films
- Heads of departments of make-up, hair and costume, sometimes called 'chiefs', join the film very early in its preparation. There is generally a greater responsibility in working with feature films, as budgets are higher and a greater level of expertise is expected. They will be expected to know how many other personnel they will need.
- Make-up artists, hairdressers and costume staff join the team when the production starts, or just before to set up. It is likely to be a longer contract of work and needs commitment.
- Freelance staff will be booked periodically, they are sometimes referred to as 'dailies', to help with guest artists and background artists (usually known as 'extras').

Commercials

Commercials are another aspect of film work. When a company wants to advertise a product they employ and work closely with a TV or film production company. As the 'client' they have final responsibility for how the advert is shot.

There are production companies that make only commercials. They generally have their own contacts for staff and, once they are confident of the standard of work and reliability they will try and work with the same people.

Productions and personnel

Job descriptions

Make-up department

The business has changed dramatically and is now predominantly freelance. Consequently, it is more difficult to assess a person's capabilities. It would be expected that the more experience a person has, the more able they are to work on complex make-up and productions. Some training is necessary for any personnel but, even then, beginning as a runner or assistant and learning as you go may be the only way to get started. However, in the freelance world your reputation goes before you and it would be risky to take on work that is not within your capabilities and experience. On the other hand, you need the experience in order to learn and progress. The best way of gaining this is to work with more experienced people and, over time, build up a good reputation.

- *Make-up assistant*: someone who has had training in TV/film make-up and hair and is in their first two years of employment. An assistant works under the direction of an experienced person.
- *Make-up artist*: someone who has had sufficient experience to enable them to work alone.
- *Make-up designer*: someone who is very experienced and capable of taking responsibility for all make-up production requirements and the budget.

Hairdressing department

- *Assistant hairdresser*: someone who has served an apprenticeship or had relevant hairdressing training and is able to work alongside others to learn about working in the film industry.
- *Hairstylist*: someone with enough experience of working in films to be able to take responsibility and work alone.
- *Head of department*: sometimes called 'chief hairstylist'. Someone who has enough experience to prepare for all production requirements, to budget and to organize department staff as necessary.

Costume department

- *Costume assistant*: sometimes called a 'dresser'. It is preferable to have some knowledge of sewing, costume design and media studies, but duties include putting out clothes, washing and ironing, and the general maintenance of the department. On larger productions, a costume assistant may have specific artists to dress and care for throughout the production, and be answerable to the supervisor or costume designer.
- *Costume supervisor*: someone experienced enough to take responsibility for the everyday running of a production, organizing staff and ensuring continuity regarding costumes.

- *Costume designer*: takes responsibility for designing the 'look' of the whole production regarding clothes and is responsible for production buying and budgeting.

Wig department
- *Wig fitter*: someone who takes head measurements and finds a suitable well-fitting wig that can be dressed into the required style. A wig fitter requires a great knowledge of working with wigs and hairstyles, both modern and period.
- *Wigmaker*: someone who makes the wig foundations from the measurements and knots the wigs. They make other postiches such as hairpieces, pincurls and facial hair.
- *Wig dresser*: dresses the wigs and hairpieces into the required style.

Job descriptions

Why have make-up, hair and costume staff?

Apart from making someone look attractive and boosting their confidence there are many reasons for employing make-up, hair and costume personnel, all of which are important.

Make-up

- To make any corrections and adjustments due to the effects of lighting.
- To balance skin tones. For example if there are two faces in close-up, one very pale and one very tanned, this is distracting and may cause difficulty in lighting the shot.
- To maintain a balanced skin tone throughout the production. This is crucial for film work, as one minute the artist may be indoors with a nice rosy complexion and the next minute outside in the snow with their face turning blue!
- To create character make-up, ranging from old age on a young face to fantasy make-up as in science fiction productions.

Hair

- To enhance and keep hair tidy and away from the face for lighting purposes.
- For continuity purposes. On a long production hair length, style and colour must be appropriate to script requirements.
- To create character and period hairstyles.

Make-up and costume staff need to stay with the artists

Costume

- To advise and make adjustments to clothes and colour for lighting purposes.
- To provide costumes and clothing for production requirements.
- To create character and period costumes.
- To provide sufficient clothing for long, ongoing productions and for artists acting as 'doubles' or stunt doubles.
- To provide sufficient warm clothing for artists working outside, sometimes in inclement weather.

Elaborate costumes designed for theatre

Why have make-up, hair and costume staff?

Make-up

The skill of a good make-up artist is that the make-up is not seen! If someone notices it, other than for professional reasons, then it has not achieved its purpose, which is to create an illusion.

An important thing to learn is to apply make-up gently and in a way that is comfortable for the subject. The best way to understand this is to have someone apply a make-up to you and notice the different pressures that people use. It is surprising how rough we can be without realizing, just moving someone's head around.

Make-up time is an important period for the artist. They are about to give a performance and they will be feeling anxious. It has become a major part of a make-up artist's job to provide a gentle, calm and relaxing environment, not just to help the artist but because an agitated artist may not be happy with the work you have done!

Get to know the feel of a brush for instance. Fingers should never be used, but having the tips of a brush put onto your skin, even a nice sable brush, can be extremely uncomfortable. Applying pencils around the eyes may be fine if you are applying them to your own, but they pull the skin easily and there are better products to use.

Equipment must be kept clean at all times, as must hands. Nothing that has been used on one face should be used on another without having been cleaned. This, of course, means having extra equipment as there will often not be the time to do this between make-ups. For reasons of hygiene, brush mascara should not be shared and cake mascaras are good to have although they are not waterproof. Lipsticks should be applied with a brush, not only for hygiene reasons but also because it produces better results.

Know your products. There are so many colours and methods of applying colour. There are powder colours, creams and greases. They all produce different effects on different coloured skins. Unless you have lots of time or know a skin well, having applied a good foundation this is not the time to experiment!

Although photographic make-up artists do work without a mirror, for TV and film it is important to learn to work from what is seen in the mirror. It is what the camera sees, and the lighting around the mirror should give a balanced picture.

A make-up artist works to one side of the artist, enabling him or her to look in the mirror constantly to check the work

The face

It is important for a make-up artist to understand the human skull and bone structure, the formation of the muscles and skin colouring. This is to understand:

1. massage techniques and to be able to work on a face without causing any discomfort;
2. the highlights and shadows caused by light and how to enhance a face;
3. why some colours are flattering to a face and others are not.

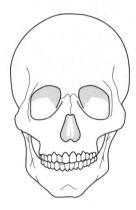

The skull

A good exercise designed to show this clearly is to paint on a face all the shadows with black make-up and all the highlights with white make-up as shown in the diagram opposite.

Drawing the face will also help you to understand its proportions. The face can be divided into equal proportions.

It can be seen that the eyes are in fact half way between the top of the head and the chin, and the nose half way between the eyes and the chin. The ears are bigger than is generally thought and are drawn between the eyes and the tip of the nose. The width of the face can also be divided into five sections each being the width of an eye

Once this 'perfect' face has been understood it can be seen more clearly how faces differ.

It is important to remember that both sides of the face are never the same. We are not 'perfect' and that is what makes each of us special and individual. When doing a corrective make-up, for instance shading a nose or jawline, try to make sure that the person does not feel that they have something wrong.

A skull-effect make-up

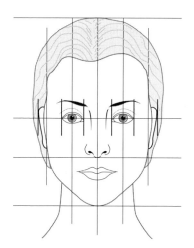

Different facial proportions

Different facial shapes

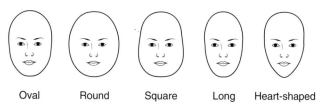

Oval   Round   Square   Long   Heart-shaped

The basics of cleansing

Whatever the colour of the skin, its texture or type, it will always benefit from a good cleansing routine. Dead cells are continually shed by the skin. Minute particles of dust, natural secretion from the sebaceous and sweat glands, and stale make-up all contribute to the blocking of pores, creating blackheads, spots and giving a 'muddy' appearance.

Cleansing is a most important procedure as it gently lifts waste matter and oils. The skin will start to look and feel fresher and will be able to function more effectively.

No matter what the treatment, any movement of the skin must be gentle and controlled. Heavy handling will stretch the skin, cause broken capillaries and overstimulate the sebaceous glands. It will damage the texture and also be uncomfortable for the artist.

Simple cleansing can be done by either applying cleansing milk or cream over the face and then removing it with cotton wool, or by applying the cleanser to damp cotton wool and then wiping the face with it.

Facial massage is usually done by standing behind the client's head and, using both hands, massaging both sides of the face simultaneously. Learning massage techniques is helpful and although there are several different techniques the basic moves are much the same, following the direction of the muscle.

Toning
Apply skin tonic or astringent to two damp pads of cotton wool and, holding one in each hand, follow the movements for cleansing. The toning action helps to remove the residues of cleanser, close pores and give the skin a good colour and a more taut appearance. Toning the skin before a make-up not only removes any grease, it is refreshing for the artist.

Moisturizing
Apply moisturizer in the same way as a facial massage routine. Whether to moisturize before a make-up depends on the skin type. Some skin does not absorb creams or grease well and the moisturizer may leave the foundation 'sitting' on the skin and more difficult to keep.

Manicure

Hands are important and often forgotten. An artist's hands may be held up against the face or there may be a close-up of the fingers holding something. In period productions particularly it is important to check whether nail varnish is being worn and whether that is appropriate.

Shape nails with an emery board. Always file from the sides towards the tip to form a curve. Do not file too low at the sides as this will cause the nails to split. When the correct shape is achieved, bevel the free edge to avoid splitting and to remove any roughness.

Apply hand cream by gentle massage. Remove residue cream around the nails with nail polish remover to eliminate any trace of grease.

Apply a polish base coat to the nails. It should be applied in three light strokes from the base to the top of the nail. Apply the first stroke in the centre of the nail and then either side, keeping away from the cuticle and skin. Remove any excess on the skin with a cotton wool-tipped orange stick dipped in nail polish remover.

Although, like false eyelashes, false nails are not used much, they are extremely useful for a make-up artist to have in their kit.

Manicure

Foundation

There are several types of foundation, all with different uses and benefits. For film and TV it is necessary to avoid too much orange in the colour as the camera is very sensitive to reds. Unless the materials are especially bought for a particular artist, a make-up artist needs to have a variety of colours and makes of foundation. It is important to know how to mix two or three colours to match different skin tones. Do not be tempted by the names of foundations. Colours must be tested on the skin. A kit can contain only so much and, in principle, six colours are all that may be needed: fair, medium and dark for white skins; fair, medium and dark for black skins. Thus, most skin tones can be catered for. However, skin tones do vary in the amount of yellow, red and blue they contain, and experience will enable a make-up artist to understand what colours are useful for mixing.

Types of foundation

- *Liquid foundation*: this is a light foundation for everyday use. As the technical quality of the cameras improved it became possible to use more natural make-up. These foundations are made for different skin types, such as moisturized for dry skin, or non-allergenic for sensitive skins, and have become popular with make-up artists as they reduce the chance of any adverse skin reaction.
- *Cream foundation*: this provides a thicker coverage although care must be taken with greasy skins. Cream foundations come in different styles, compacts, pots and sticks. Some are designed for everyday use, others, with more pigment, for TV and stage use. There is also a type with added powder, although when working under lights, loose powder will often still need to be used.

Cream foundations in different containers, depending on the amount of pigment

A selection of grease foundations

- *Grease foundation*: these are designed for stage work. The advantage of grease make-up is that it provides a good base when a lot of shading is required. It is useful therefore for character make-up, but it does require a great deal of powdering.
- *Camouflage make-up*: this is a grease make-up in many subtle shades of greens, yellows and reds. It is very high in pigment to give greater coverage of the skin. It is designed to disguise skin imperfections such as burns or scars but is extremely useful for covering unwanted freckles or liver spots caused by ageing.
- *Pancake foundation*: these are powder based and therefore water-soluble. They are quick to use as they don't need extra powdering. However, they produce a very flat effect and so are seldom used on faces. They are useful for body make-up; particularly for necks and shoulders that are likely to catch the light and so need the extra powder.

  There are now cake foundations that combine a cream base with powder. They are quick to use and are intended to be used without extra powder; however, for working under lights they often do need extra powder. They give good coverage but can look very 'flat'.
- *Aquacolours*: these are water based and come in many lovely colours. They are used for face and body painting and fantasy make-up.

Applying the foundation

A foundation is not simply a make-up base. It is the foundation for all your work. It gives a smooth, even tone to the skin. Natural skin is made up of a number of colours: reds and yellows and even blues. Cameras are getting better all the time and are now considerably more true to colour, but they are still more sensitive to some colours, reds especially, than others. Any reds in the skin will be emphasized, and blue will appear as shadows, e.g. around the eyes. A camera seems to exaggerate any imperfections and this is why any 'straight' make-up, i.e. natural, everyday make-up, done for the camera will include corrective measures. Even if the artist has an ideal skin, it is likely she or he will need a foundation for these reasons. A very pale skin may need a little more colour, for instance, and it is important for black skins not to have a foundation darker than their natural tone but preferably one lighter, for lighting purposes.

Men may not want a foundation and they do tend to have stronger skin tones, but it will be necessary if they have a strong beard line. The camera will pick out the blue and it will look as though they are unshaven. It will be necessary to apply a foundation to this area that will need to be blended into the natural skin tone.

Foundation is applied with a damp sponge. First, this is more hygienic and feels more pleasant. Second, a smoother and more even finish can be achieved. There are several types of sponge, natural and synthetic, and although a natural sponge is more supple, it is a matter of personal preference which is used.

Generally, a make-up artist will use a palette with a little foundation on it. This is so that the colour can be mixed. For speed's sake, the palette is usually the back of their other hand, and care must be taken not to spill foundation over the artist! A good place to start application is on the forehead to judge the tone, and on down the nose. When working around the eyes care must be taken, not only for the comfort of the artist, but also because the skin there is very delicate. The artist may also be wearing contact lenses.

It is important to learn to apply foundation well. It must be even and blended well around the hairline, neck and ears. It is very noticeable on camera if the neck is a lighter shade than the face, and the camera picks up a lot of red in the ears. Another problem to watch for is red flushes that appear on an artist's neck due to anxiety. A foundation with a greater pigment content may have to be used on this area. The foundation is the basis of the whole make-up and if it is not done well the whole effect will be spoiled.

Blending

Blending is an important element of a good make-up and must be practised to perfection. It is this that creates the illusion and, if hard edges are left, it is seen more obviously as make-up.

■ *Foundation*: with a damp sponge apply a dark foundation onto the skin. The inside of the arm is a good place to practise. Smooth away the colour so that the change in colour is barely noticeable. Practise this both with the sponge and with large brushes.
■ *Cream or grease colours*: as above, practise with smaller brushes blending the colour so that there are no hard edges.
■ *Powder colours*: apply the colour to the skin with a dry brush and use a clean, dry brush to blend away the edges. The colour can be made stronger by successive applications and colours can be blended into one another. Powder colours do have a tendency to 'drop', to fall onto the cheekbones for instance if using eye colours. Generally the better the quality of product, the less it will spread.

The colour is blended away to leave no 'edges'

Airbrushing

Airbrushing is a technique of putting paint or make-up into a pressurized container and spraying it onto an object or skin. The method is quick but obviously has limitations when it comes to applying make-up. It can be useful when used for body-painting.

Foundation

Powder

Powder is used for setting the make-up. It comes in compacts or as loose powder and there are a variety of colours. It also comes as a standard grade or as a fine powder called translucent powder. This is most commonly used for professional work as it gives a more natural look. It is helpful if the powder blends with the colour of the foundation, but a light, translucent powder has no colour and will not affect the colour of the foundation. This powder can be used on any skin tone.

The main thing to remember about powdering a face is that too much will exaggerate any small lines. If the face needs heavy powdering to set the make-up well, try to avoid too much around the eyes. The area likely to need the heaviest powdering is the central section from the forehead, down the nose and around the mouth.

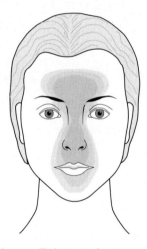

The central area of the face is more likely to need extra powdering under hot lights

For light powdering a large, soft powder brush can be used, but for powder to last and set the make-up a velour puff should be used. The powder should be carefully but firmly pressed into the skin, not rubbed. Any excess can be brushed off with a powder brush. It is important again to take care around the eyes, especially if contact lenses are being worn.

There are compressed powders that are very quick and easy to use. They come in a variety of colours but only a few will be suitable for TV and film use. They give good coverage if someone needs a little colour quickly and the translucent variety is extremely useful.

As a camera will pick up any shine because of the heavy lights, powder may need to be reapplied regularly throughout the production. If a man has a good skin tone, powder may be all the make-up he needs. It may be, because there is no time, that it is the minimum anyone has. Powder and a velour puff are a make-up person's best friend!

Colours for eyes and cheeks now come in powder form and tend to be more popular as cosmetic houses make small compacts containing several complementary colours.

A selection of powder make-up

Eyes and cheeks

Eye shadows and blushers, sometimes known as 'rouge', come in creams, grease or powders. If grease or cream is being used it would obviously be applied before powdering. Powder colours, added after powdering the foundation, are possibly more convenient as they can be built up slowly to the required effect and can be refreshed more easily as the day goes on. For TV and film work the amount of shine in the product is significant: any shine or glitter will catch the lights and will only be useful for certain effects.

There are many colours to choose from. Whether you are picking up the colour of the artist's eyes or clothes, colours are generally mixed and blended. Colours for black skins need to contain more pigment for better coverage; they need warmer colours too, colours with more orange and yellow in them, although lilacs look lovely.

Although cream blushers can be applied with a sponge, colours are generally applied with brushes. Remember that the first stroke of colour will be the strongest, so work from the outside in; the strongest colour on eyes will be at the outside corner, and for blusher the strongest colour will be nearest the hairline. There are various brush sizes for this work. Blusher brushes tend to be bigger, rounder and softer to give more subtle effects. Clean brushes can be used for blending.

Eyes
When shaping eyes, the aim is to make them as open and almond shaped as possible. The ideal is to have a balance between the eyelid, socket line and under the brows.

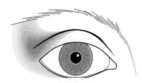

A well balanced eye. The natural socket line divides the eyelid and the eyebone in good proportions. To enhance this, use a lighter shade on the lid and follow the socket line with a darker complementary colour

When there is less eyelid showing, this area will have to be lightened as much as possible. This can also be helped by shading a darker socket line higher than it is to give the illusion of less space under the brows.

Otherwise eye make-up is very much geared to fashion and the type of make-up required for the work. Soft brown and beige colours will give a delicate, natural look while bright turquoise or pink colours are lovely for fashion or fantasy make-up.

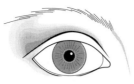

For an eye with a heavier eyebone, light the eyelid as much as possible and keep the heavier shading on the eyebone above the natural socket line. This will appear to 'lift' the outer corner

Right

Wrong

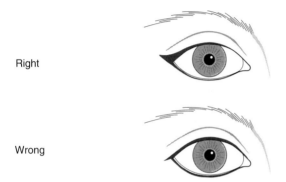

An eyeline. When doing an eyeline it is more flattering to accentuate the outer corner of the eye and be careful to lift the 'tail' end. If the outside corner drops it can give the sense of ageing or sadness. If the eyeline is too heavy at the inner corner of the eye it will be too distracting

1. Very strong highlight to give appearance of heavy inner lid

2. Keep inner brow straight and low

3. Strong eyeline – dark and thin at inner corner, thick and lifted at outer corner

4. Heavier shading at outer corner of eye

5. Keep outer brow high

Shading can be used to change the shape of the eye slightly, e.g. to give an oriental look

Cheeks

Rouge or blusher on cheeks is for contouring or giving the illusion of higher cheekbones and to put back into the face the colour evened out by the foundation. For more natural make-up a brown shade just under the cheekbones may be all that is needed. A pinker shade can be used just on the cheekbone to give colour. For black skins, strong rusty colours are good.

For men who have a full foundation, a browner shade brushed on the cheekbone will put colour back into their face.

Natural blushers need not be limited to cheekbones. A light dusting of colour can be put onto temples, foreheads and around chins to soften and give warmth to faces. A brown-toned blusher can also be used for brushing around the jawline and 'double chins' to give some shading.

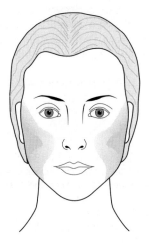

Cheeks. The strongest colour will be right under the cheekbones by the hairline, to give the impression of higher cheekbones. Generally under lights the cheekbones do not need to be highlighted

Lashes, brows and lips

These are the finishing touches to make-up.

Mascara

There are several types of mascara for lashes and several colours, including blue. Some mascaras claim to lengthen or thicken lashes and artists usually have their own favourites. For reasons of hygiene, it is preferable to use the artist's own, but that is not always possible. There is a cake mascara that is mixed with water and comes with a special mascara brush. This is obviously not waterproof, so it is not suitable if the script calls for the artist to cry.

Mascara is generally accepted as a necessary part of a woman's make-up but for men who have light coloured lashes or brows it is equally important. Under heavy lights, fair hair tends to 'disappear'. Lashes, brows and sometimes even the hairline need to be darkened and cake mascara is useful for this; it colours the hair rather than the skin, which a pencil is more likely to do.

Filling in eyebrows and giving them a good shape can also be done with a cake eyeliner or dark powder eye shadow.

False eyelashes

False lashes are used now mostly for period productions or character work. They can be applied in strip form or as individual lashes.

To apply strip lashes, apply surgical adhesive to the lash strip. Allow it to become tacky and then place the strip as near as possible to the lash line, using tweezers as an aid if necessary. The outside corner of the lashes can be lifted a little to 'open' the eye. An eyeliner is used to cover the base of the lashes.

Individual lashes give a more natural look. Surgical adhesive is applied to the 'root' end of the lash, which is then attached to the natural lash as close to the lid as possible. The false lashes will 'grow out' with the natural lashes. Try to avoid using mascara as this cannot easily be removed without removing the lashes too!

Lipstick

There is a huge range of lipsticks available and it is a matter of personal choice, but matching the overall colours well is important. Lipsticks are usually applied with a brush. This is hygienic but also enables a more accurate outline to be drawn. Lips can also be outlined with lip pencils. This may stop the colour bleeding and spreading, or can be used just to give definition to the lips. Except for character make-up, it is advisable not to try to change the shape of the lips too much; the camera is likely to be sensitive to the change of tones.

Tinting brows and lashes

It may be necessary on a long-running production to shape and tint brows and lashes for continuity purposes.

Eyebrow shaping

To shape eyebrows, work under a good light and use a pair of tweezers that meet well at the tip.

Remove all the make-up on or under the brow. Wipe the brow with toning tonic. This should also be done during the procedure to remove stray hairs and cool the brow. Gently stretch the skin between two fingers and pluck the hairs in the direction of growth. Hair should mainly be removed from below the brow. Stray hairs between the brows and the temples may be removed so long as they do not form part of the main arch. Strong, long or discoloured hairs in the brow may be removed if their removal does not alter the brow line.

Tinting

Eyebrows help to emphasize facial expression and eyelashes frame the eyes. Both can be tinted. The tint will last as long as the lashes, that is about six weeks, and tints are available in black, brown and grey. Two colours may be blended to give a muted colour as required.

Contra indications: eyelash and brow tinting should not be done if:

1. there is a history of eye sensitivity or allergy;
2. there are septic areas or broken skin.

Eyebrows

Cleanse the eye area with a mild tonic. Surround the eyebrow with a little petroleum jelly. Mix a little of the tint according to the instructions, approximately a quarter of an inch with two or three drops of hydrogen peroxide.

The tint can be applied with a fine brush or an orange stick covered with cotton wool. Apply first to the under hairs and then the top hairs shaping the brow line. Remove excess tint with damp cotton wool and ensure none remains on the skin.

Check for colour density after three to five minutes. Blond hair colours rapidly and over-tinting will give a very harsh appearance. Red hair may take longer to colour. Dark hair will require only a little tint at the ends to even the shading. Ensure that the tint is left on both brows for the same length of time.

Eyelashes

Apply petroleum jelly in a line on both upper and lower eyelids close to the lashes but not touching the roots. Place shaped pads of damp cotton wool under both eyes.

Apply the tint using a brush or thin orange stick tipped with cotton wool over the upper and lower lashes, working outwards from the roots to the tips.

Cover each eye with two pads of damp cotton wool, one on the eyelid and one below the eye. This helps keep the tint warm and also helps the artist relax so they do not open their eyes. Test for colour after five to ten minutes. When the desired tone is achieved, remove both the pads together in a firm, even movement from the outer to the inner corner of the eye. This will remove most of the tint. Remove any remaining tint with damp cotton wool.

False eyelashes

Tinting brows and lashes

Straight corrective make-up

It is important to realize that the use of lighting and cameras affects the make-up.

Shading and highlighting

After many hours of studying faces on a screen, a make-up artist learns to recognize these effects. For example, top lighting will exaggerate any shadows on the face, such as under the eyes and the nose-to-mouth lines. These are the areas that generally need highlighting.

The principles of highlighting and shading are:

- lightening an area on the skin will bring it forward, therefore highlight a feature or lighten a shadow;
- alleviating lines and shadows on the face will give the effect of health and youth;
- shading an area will push it back, creating a shadow;
- shading in already sunken areas will create the illusion of ill health and ageing;
- highlighting and shading can appear to change the shape of a face. For example, if a face is round, highlighting the cheekbones and shading the jaw line will make the face appear slimmer.

Any shading and highlighting is applied after the foundation.

Highlighting involves using a colour lighter than the base colour or just adding white to the foundation that is being used. Highlighting is generally applied with a brush so that it can be blended well. Spots or red marks can be covered with concealer or cover-up cream. Concealers are foundations with more pigment in them and usually come in smaller tubes or pots. As they have more pigment they give better cover, although if the spot is also a bump you can only take out the colour – the 'bump' will still catch the light. There is only so much that we can do with make-up!

If the artist looks straight into the mirror, the deepest shadows will be revealed. If in doubt, move the artist's head down and the shadows will be exaggerated. Remember that the first strokes of the brush or sponge will hold most make-up and produce the deepest colour, so start where you want the depth of colour. In highlighting the eyes this would be in the inside corner of the eyes under the brows and again just under the bags under the eyes. This can be blended away with a clean brush. Some people just have a dark skin colouring under the eyes which is easy to highlight. Others have 'bags under the eyes', an area which must not be highlighted as this will exaggerate the 'bags'. Only the creases or deep shadows must be highlighted. Points to look out for:

- pale skins may need a warmer base;
- do not use a darker base on black skins;
- fringes and deep-set eyes will cause shadows. Keep the eyes light;

- beard lines will appear darker on camera. Apply a base or covering powder;
- fair eyebrows and lashes may 'disappear'. Fill in with dark shadow, pencil or mascara.

Make-up notes

On ongoing productions, even for a straight make-up, it is important to keep notes, not only of what was done but the colours used and any changes in hairstyle or ornaments used. It may be that the scene has to be re-shot at a later date or that the make-up artist is sick and someone else has to take over the work. Any continuity photos can be pinned to the notes.

ARTIST – Anne Smith
 	
CHARACTER – Mrs Jones
 	
Mother – wears little m/up
	Make – up
	Foundation – Warm Beige
	Highlighting – under eyes
	Shading – around jaw line
	Eyes – beige on lid
	             – brown in socket line
	             – brown mascara
	             – fill in brows –Taupe
	Cheeks – Crushed Peach
	Lips – Natural Spice
	
	Hair
	Set in heated rollers

Day 1. Sc. 2. – Early morning Sc. 3. – Shopping	Untidy hair. No lipstick Scarf used as hair band
Day 2. Sc. 1. Eve. Restaurant	Hair dressed up with gold slide Lipstick – Rhubarb

Make-up notes for an artist appearing in three scenes over two days

Ageing make-up

The principles of lightening and shading discussed in the last section are used for ageing but instead of correcting shadows and unwanted lines these are deliberately exaggerated. The bone structure does not change in the ageing process, but the muscles around it become less elastic and fall to create wrinkles.

The skin also becomes finer, showing veins and small broken blood vessels. Any blue around the eyes becomes more noticeable. Small, dark patches, called liver spots, appear and when the skin tans it may stay patchy. Black skins particularly show dark patches when ageing. These are the effects that need to be created or exaggerated.

Each face is individual and will age differently. It will be no good trying to hollow the cheeks of a round, chubby face! You need to study the face in the mirror. Tilting the chin down will give clues as the lighting around the mirror shows up the shadows and creases in the face. Asking the artist to smile will show up the 'laughter lines' around both the eyes and mouth. Moving the skin gently and feeling the bone structure beneath will indicate how that particular face will age.

How strong the make-up needs to be will depend on the production. For a theatre production the make-up can be quite obvious from the front of the theatre as it needs to be seen at the back. For TV and film, make-up has to be very subtle, i.e. blended away carefully so that it is not obviously make-up. Here, greying the hair is helpful and reducing the colour a little in skin tone and

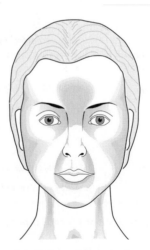

Application. After applying a foundation a darker shading colour is used to emphasize any hollowed or sunken areas. These will be at the temples, in the centre of the forehead, under the cheeks, the eye sockets, nose-to-mouth lines and jowls. The shading can be applied with a sponge or a large brush and needs to be blended into the foundation

lips too. Hands and neck are also important and should not be forgotten! A little shading and emphasizing of the blue veins will make all the difference.

Cream or grease foundation is easier to work with. The make-up will move more easily and blending will be more effective. Mixing the shading colours will also be easier with grease make-up. There are specific shading colours, but it is better to have a palette of several colours to be able to match the colour more accurately with the skin tone. Some skins have more yellow in them than others, for instance. Browns and grey-blue colours can be mixed to give good effect.

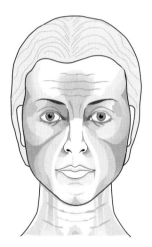

With a small brush and a darker shading still, exaggerate the deepest points and any wrinkles. With a clean brush blend any sharp edges. The ageing process can be built up in this way to the appropriate look. However, there will be a point when the make-up will start to be obvious and for TV and film this will not be acceptable

Ageing make-up using special effects

It may be that the use of make-up alone will not achieve the full effect of ageing. There are products that can be painted on the skin that cause it to wrinkle. Latex is the base. It is a clear liquid that dries quickly forming a fine layer of 'skin' over the appropriate areas. The drying can be speeded by using a hair-dryer on a cool setting, taking care not to make the artist uncomfortable. To exaggerate the wrinkles, the skin is stretched a little while the latex (which has been lightly powdered) is drying. When the skin is relaxed it will then wrinkle. A little latex used carefully around the eyes is extremely effective.

Great care must be taken around the eyes. A barrier cream should be applied first, but it would be as well to do a skin test: try a little of the product on some sensitive skin, such as behind the ears.

Points to remember:

- work with care. Protect clothes with a wrap; protect eyelashes with petroleum jelly, making sure your artist is comfortable;
- know exactly where to apply the latex. Study the face and see where it will effectively wrinkle. Use less rather than more as, being a second 'skin', it can look shiny and false;

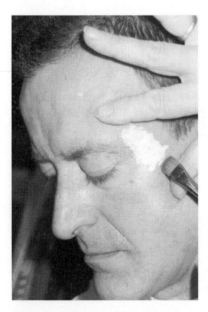

Applying ageing latex to a small area. This can also be stippled on with a sponge, but use an old sponge that can be thrown away

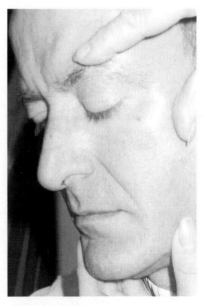

Hold the skin stretched while the latex dries. A cool hairdryer will help this process

- pour a little latex in a bowl. Latex dries quickly once exposed to air, so replace tops on bottles and use only small amounts;
- add powder colour to the latex before using. Although the application should be very thin, latex does dry slightly light and dark skins may need some extra colour;
- use a sponge to apply the latex; as it dries so quickly it will ruin your brushes. Cut a cheap sponge into several pieces that can be thrown away;
- stretch the skin in the direction of the natural line on the face;
- stipple small areas at a time, keeping the edges fine;
- when dry, powder lightly before releasing the skin;
- if a lot of ageing is required, don't forget the neck and hands;
- when finished, the make-up can be completed. The wrinkles should be adequate in themselves. It should not be necessary to do a lot of extra shading.

Removing the latex must be done gently. There are specific manufactured products, but damp cotton wool will lift the edges slowly. The skin may be a little sore if the make-up has been on for a long time.

There are ageing products that are water-soluble. However, it is important to know what the script requires the artist to do. Also, if the artist is prone to excessive perspiration, the make-up could start to lift.

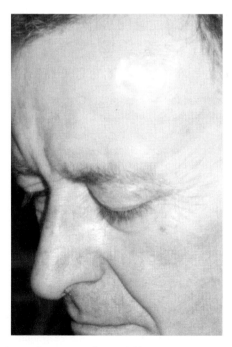

Allow the skin to relax and encourage it to wrinkle

Character make-up

As with ageing, most character make-up is done with creams or grease paints so that the work can be done with ease: the make-up 'moves' more easily and changes to it can be made as you go along.

Character make-up can be 'copied', as in clown make-up, or can be personally designed to suit the character or fantasy.

The important thing is the application of the different materials.

1. If any special effects such as prosthetics, latex or wax are being used, they should be applied to clean skin before the foundation. It must be remembered that make-up applied to anything other than real skin will reflect or absorb light differently. On camera, latex, foam or wax pieces will appear a different colour, generally paler, so will need a darker foundation. The whole make-up must, therefore, be checked on camera.
2. The foundation is applied and then any shading and lighting.
3. If liquid, cream or grease foundations have been used, powdering now takes place before any water-based make-up, such as eyeliner, and aquacolours.
4. If false eyelashes are being used, they are generally applied before the eyeliner.
5. Powder eye shadows or blushers are applied.
6. Once the make-up is complete, facial hair can be added if required. Hair lace sticks better to clean skin so it may be necessary to avoid applying foundation to these areas. Gluing hair lace is important. Some glues are shiny; a matt glue is preferable for TV and film. Press onto the skin with a damp powder puff or face cloth to prevent too much make-up or dirt being caught on the hair lace.
7. Wigs can now be added and hairstyles created to complete the effect.
8. Don't forget the neck and hands!

For period make-up, it is necessary to do some research and make notes. There are plenty of books on the subject and museums are great places to visit for information. If there is something specific needed, often a librarian will help to search for it.

Aquacolours are pressed powder colours that are mixed with water and painted on as you would use paints. They can come in individual pots or in palettes of mixed colours. They give a very 'flat' appearance to the make-up and are therefore better suited to fantasy make-ups. Some of the colours are lovely and some even have glitter added.

Fantasy make-up really allows you to be creative. Designing the make-up first on paper, or computer if you have the resources, will save a lot of time and give you confidence. Clown make-up and face painting for children will give you practice at working on both sides of the face. Both sides need to be symmetrical, which does take practice.

Most make-up artists will say that period and character make-up make all the hard work worthwhile! It is the most exciting and rewarding part of the job.

Character make-up is fun to do

Hair

Crêpe hair

The cheapest false hair is crêpe hair, which is made from wool. Long strands of wool are brushed and plaited into long wefts and then dyed. When it is being used, it is cut to length and teased out into fluffy strands or balls of 'hair'. This is generally used for wig dressing when the hairstyle requires more body or width than the wig can provide. The crêpe hair is used as 'stuffing'. It can be straightened by removing the cord, wetting the braided hair and stretching it to dry.

In the theatre or for fun or fantasy make-up, crêpe hair can be used to create beards and moustaches. It can be dyed any colour or sprayed with coloured hair dyes. Spirit gum is applied to the area to be covered and the crêpe hair laid on the gum using a metal tool to prevent it sticking to fingers.

Lengths of crêpe hair plaited onto string, cut to required length and 'teased' out

Real hair

Animal hair, e.g. yak hair, is the least expensive of real hair and is used for making facial hair and body hair. It is treated and dyed in various colours.

Human hair used for wigs and hairpieces is of European or Asian origin, the latter being less expensive. Human hair is still treated, bleached and dyed but it retains its natural structure. There are hair manufacturers who buy and prepare all kinds of hair. When hair is dyed it is all one colour, which makes it look unnatural, especially on camera, so different coloured hair is blended to give a natural overall colour. There may be three or four colours blended to produce a natural shade of blonde, brown or even grey.

Hair is sold in bundles, always tied at the roots so that it can be used correctly. Natural hair has scales that lie in the direction of growth, i.e. from the roots to the tips. It is vital that when hair is being used for any type of wig the scales are all lying in the same direction. If they are not, they will rub against each other and will not lie smoothly together. This will make the wig extremely difficult to keep well dressed as the hair will always 'creep' against itself, causing knots and tangles that will be difficult to dress out again.

Bundles of hair tied at the root end

Mixing hair

A hackle is used for mixing hair, which is a skilled process. Small sections of hair in several shades are held together at the root ends. The hair is then flicked into the hackle and drawn out leaving some hair behind. When there is sufficient hair in the hackle it is drawn out by the roots and added to the main bundle again. This process is repeated until the hair is sufficiently mixed. Care should be taken to tie the bundle of hair again at the roots to ensure correct use.

Different colours of hair are flicked through a hackle for mixing

The mixed hair is held between drawing mats so that it can be pulled out a few hairs at a time

Powdered wigs

Powdered wigs are sometimes made with white crêpe hair. If they are meant to look like very good authentic wigs, real hair is used and a white powder is moistened and combed right through the finished wig. When set such a wig is very 'solid'.

The last touches to a powdered wig

Facial hair

Facial hair is made by wigmakers, the hair being knotted onto hair lace and dressed. The hair is usually a mixture of human hair and yak hair, colours being mixed to give a natural effect.

The hair will lie in the direction of the knot so it is important that the lace is knotted in the direction that the hair grows.

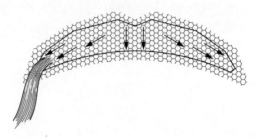

A pattern for a moustache showing the direction of the growth

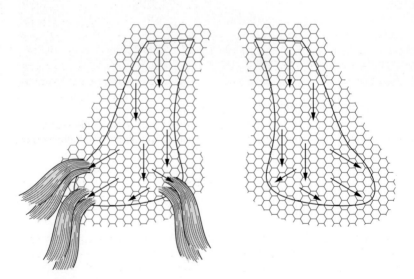

A pattern for sideboards

Applying facial hair
Moustaches are stuck down completely to keep them secure when the face moves. Most of a beard, certainly all around the hair lace edge, also needs to be stuck down. Where the sideboards meet the hairline, the natural hair is lifted

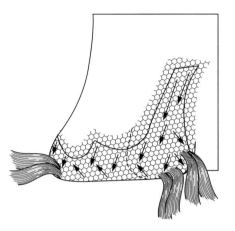

A pattern for beards

and the false hair tucked underneath. The hair is then combed and blended into the sideboard. A mirror is required to make sure the hairpiece is centred in line with the chin.

1. Unless it is necessary to apply make-up under the lace it is preferable that the skin is free of grease – otherwise the hair lace may not stick well. When new, the lace will need to be trimmed to fit the artist's face. It is best not to cut the lace too close to the hair. Once cut it cannot be replaced and it is useful to have sufficient lace to trim again as it wears. It is advisable to cut the lace edge slightly unevenly. If the edge is too straight it may be more difficult to disguise or may pull as the face moves.
2. Apply spirit gum to the area and wait for it to become a little tacky.
3. Apply the facial hair, using the mirror to see that it is centred with the nose and meets the ears correctly.
4. Use a damp cloth or powder puff to press the lace into the gum.
5. Where the sideboard meets the hairline, lift the natural hair with a comb and tuck the false hair underneath. The natural hair is then combed and blended into the sideboard.

It is important to study the colouring of facial hair. It is not uncommon to have several different colours on the same face. Blond men often have red sideboards; also sideboards can be quite grey while the head of hair is still dark.

Dressing facial hair

There are malleable chin blocks for the dressing of false facial hair. The piece is secured to the block with blocking pins and blocking tape or galloon. The hair is then lifted, cut to the length and shape required if necessary, curled with hot moustache tongs and combed into shape.

Special moustache tongs are used, which come in several sizes. They need a specific type of heater; some have only one heater, some have two, one hotter than the other. These tongs require practice and skill to use. They are held in the hand as shown. Hair is quite resilient and can withstand a lot of heat. Therefore, the tongs must be quite hot. However, if they are too hot, the hair will singe. If the hair is burnt it will break off. If uncertain, use a tissue to test the heat. If the tissue turns brown, the tongs are too hot!

The principle in dressing the hair is to lift it at the roots to make it look as though it is growing. Hair does grow outwards from the skin; it does not lie flat even in cool temperatures. It also grows in a particular direction, so it is important to understand hair growth.

Open the tongs and pick up a small section of hair across the direction of growth. Close the tongs and pull upwards away from the lace and in the direction of 'growth' at a speed that allows the hair to curl in the heat of the tongs.

Re-heat the tongs and pick up another section. Continue until all the hair is lifted and curled. When the hair has cooled and is combed back into position, it will look like natural facial hair. Experience will show how much curl is needed to look realistic.

See also page 132 (Marcel tongs and waving).

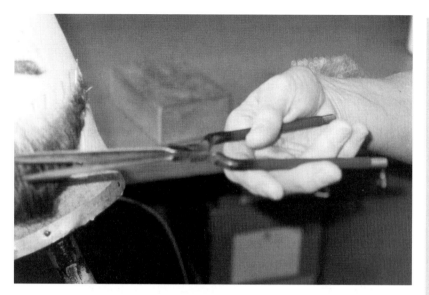

The tongs are held in the hand so that the lower fingers can open and close them while the thumb and forefinger keep them steady

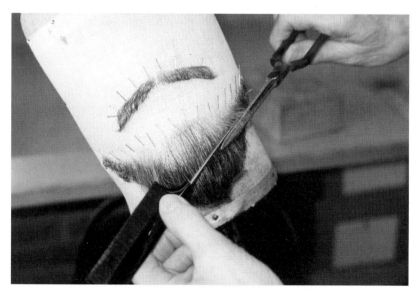

A section of hair is picked up by the tongs and the heat lifts and curls it

Removal and cleaning of facial hair

The easiest way to remove any lace and spirit gum is with a sable brush and surgical spirit. The brush can get between the lace and skin, lifting the lace without damaging it too much. The life span of facial hair is greater than wig hair lace. This is mainly because it does not matter so much when it stretches. The piece is smaller and the face flatter. The edge of the piece can be made to fit.

When cleaning facial hair, the hair lace should not be treated too roughly. The piece can be soaked in surgical spirit for a while before being placed on some tissue. The inside of the lace can then be tapped with a toothbrush or stipple brush to remove any remaining gum. The surgical spirit will dry quickly and should not disturb the dressing of the piece too much.

Alternatively, a small pad of cotton wool wrapped in muslin can be used for cleaning lace. This is also useful for cleaning spirit gum from a face. Cotton wool on its own can stick to stubble and be difficult to remove.

Sideboards to match the wig colouring complete the picture

Hollywoodian beard

Petit goatee beard

Medium full beard

Lincolnic beard

Many shapes of beards

Many shapes of moustaches

There are so many styles for beards, moustaches and sideboards that wigmakers have numbered pictures from which to choose

Creating stubble

Obviously it would be more satisfactory for an artist to grow his own stubble, but sometimes that is not possible.

A light unshaven effect can be obtained by sponging a blue-grey make-up base into the beard line. It is important to follow the natural beard line and the heavier the make-up the heavier the effect of stubble. If it has to be more realistic, perhaps for a close-up, a stubble can be applied.

- cut up some dark hair very finely into a bowl;
- darken the beard line with make-up;
- apply some stubble paste or wax to the skin, beginning underneath;
- with a soft powder brush, pick up some of the fine hairs from the bowl and place them onto the wax;
- continue to build and shape the stubble in this way.

For extremely close shots, the stubble can be pushed onto the skin through some hair lace so that as the lace is lifted off the small pieces of hair stand up as though growing from the skin.

Follow the natural beard line with make-up or stubble paste and finely chopped hair. Watch for the thinner natural hair growth around the edge of the beard line. Evenness is very important to look realistic. The lighter the application the better

Laying on hair

Sometimes it is necessary to lay the hair straight onto the face with spirit gum. This may be to cover the hair lace edges of sideboards or a beard, but it may also be to create a whole moustache. It is very time-consuming and not an easy process. It needs a great deal of practice.

- Place hair between two drawing mats, roots protruding, so that a little hair can be drawn at a time.
- Hold the hair close to the roots between the fingers and thumb of the non-dominant hand.
- Apply spirit gum to a small section of the skin.
- Catch three or four hairs and press the roots of the hair onto the gum using a metal tool or the edge of a pair of scissors to prevent sticking to fingers and the hair being pulled off again accidentally.
- Holding the tool in place, carefully pull away any hair that has not stuck.
- Working from the underneath upwards, lay on more hair in this way forming the shape required.
- Cut the hair to the length required.
- Very carefully, tong with small Marcel tongs.

Laying on hair is extremely useful if you need to add a few grey hairs into an actor's own beard. Grey hair can also be added to the hairline and eyebrows.

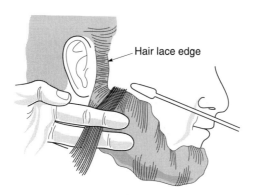

Hair lace edge

Laying on a few hairs at a time to cover hair lace

To create a whole beard and moustache by laying on hair is a skilled and time-consuming job, but this method is most useful in covering a hard and noticeable lace edge

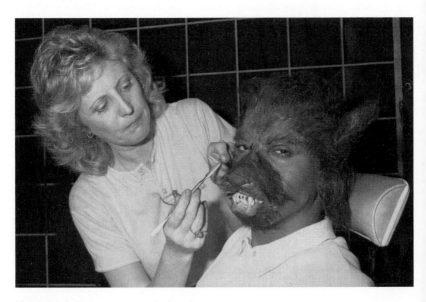

Hair being laid on over a prosthetics piece

The moustache was laid on completely for Jeremy Irons in 'A French Lieutenant's Woman' for comfort

Modern hairdressing

Before heated rollers and electric tongs were invented, artists had to arrive at studios very early to have their hair washed and set in rollers. Unless it is for something special, that is no longer necessary. Artists are expected, sometimes asked, to arrive with clean hair, and any setting is done with heated rollers or tongs.

It takes longer to train in hairdressing than make-up and takes a lot of practice and experience to make hair do what you want it to do! However experienced you are, remember to be firm and positive about what you are doing; there's nothing worse than having someone dressing your hair when they are really afraid to touch it! Most people enjoy having their hair brushed and when hair is looking nice there is a great sense of well-being.

Studying face shapes and understanding how the shape of a hairstyle can change the face is extremely important.

Blow-drying the hair

Short hair on men and women can be dried using a hairbrush and dryer. The hair is lifted with the brush in one hand while the hairdryer 'sets' it in that position. Different people have different preferences for brushes and techniques. It is extremely effective and quicker than using tongs. It gives lift to the hair, and is necessary if an artist is caught out in the rain and you need to dress the hair again.

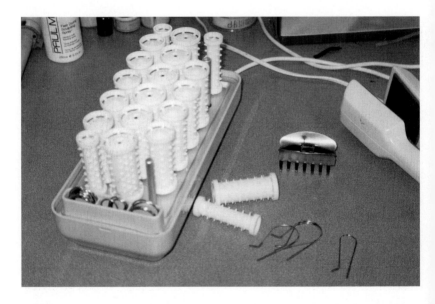

Heated rollers

There are several makes and styles, but it is worth noting how well rollers are likely to stay in. Most have spikes on the rollers and some have a foam covering. Points to remember:

- the hair should be clean and dry and worked in sections;
- to be effective, not too much hair should be put in the roller;
- for maximum root movement, comb the hair upwards and away from the direction of growth;
- check the rollers and pins are not pulling, or sticking into the head;
- the hair can be sprayed with a setting agent so long as it doesn't get too wet. It may be better to spray the head when all the rollers are in place;
- after removing the rollers, brush through the whole head of hair. If the set is good, the hair will bounce back again.

Heated tongs

- As with rollers, there are different sizes and styles. Care must be taken when using tongs with spikes that hold the hair. If the hair is very long, it can get caught and be difficult to unravel. If this does happen, unplug the tongs and take time to unravel the hair.
- Tongs are useful to lift the hair at the roots. The hair can be held securely and lifted away from the direction of growth.
- Modern tongs are particularly useful for period hairdressing, although Marcel tongs give better results. There are also tongs for straightening and for crimping hair. Spiral tongs make quick ringlets.

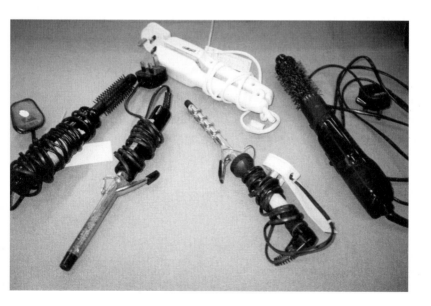

Setting hair

Whether setting wet hair in rollers or setting dry hair in heated rollers the most important thing is to create 'lift' at the roots. The rollers are generally inserted in the direction of the hair growth. If the rollers have been put in correctly and firmly, in principle any style can then be dressed. Larger rollers are used at the top of the head as the hair is longer and the amount of curl required is less.

When the hair is too short for a roller or when a tighter curl is required, the hair can be set in pincurls. The hair is wound into a curl and secured with a hairclip.

Wet setting is usually used for wigs as they need a much firmer and tighter set than natural growing hair. Once set, a net is placed over the wig or hairpiece and it is placed in a postiche oven to bake.

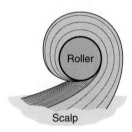

Right. The hair is taken forwards at the roots

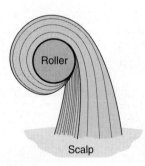

Wrong. The hair will not have so much lift and bounce

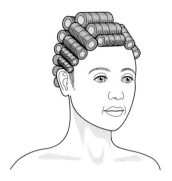

A full head dressed in rollers. Smaller rollers are used at the side and nape to give more curl

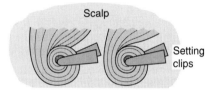

Scalp

Setting clips

A pincurl

When setting wigs, large setting pins can be used in the block to hold the curls

Styling

Understanding how natural hair falls is an important prerequisite to being able to create hairstyles. Root direction varies depending on the part of the head and from person to person. If the natural parting for someone is on the left, the style will need to follow this, with the bulk of the hair falling to the right. Going against the root movement may be uncomfortable for the wearer and the style is likely to collapse or drop out quickly.

Handling natural hair will tell an experienced dresser whether the hair is thick or fine, i.e. the fineness of the actual hair follicle, not the fineness of the head of hair. You can have a thick head of fine hair or a head of hair that is thin but with hair follicles that are thick and easier to manage. Fine hair is generally harder to manage because it is slippery and often straighter. The amount of natural curl in the hair needs to be taken into consideration also. This will help determine the tightness of the setting.

The hair needs to be brushed through firmly first. If the set was good there will be plenty of bounce and the hair can be dressed into the style required. A smaller brush or a comb can then be used for 'teasing' the hair into place.

Here the hair is curled and allowed to fall naturally but the filming is out of doors so the hair has been gripped off the face for security.

Dressing hair

When dressing hair, be brave and brush completely through the hair without worrying at this stage about the style. It feels very good to have your hair brushed like this after having it set and the hair needs to blend and lose its sections. The hair can then be combed and styled as required.

If the hair still breaks into sections or the style needs some height or thickness, the hair can be 'teased' and encouraged to keep its shape. Take some hair and from the underneath of the section, comb the hair back towards the roots. This is the same technique as backcombing but done much more gently so as to have control over where the hair falls.

Waterproof hair lacquer is a necessary item for a media make-up or hairdressing department for several reasons:

1. the style needs to keep its shape for long periods;
2. the artist may be changing clothes, which could disturb the hair;
3. the style may be subjected to inclement weather.

Modern hairdressing for film and TV may still require working with hairpieces.

A strip of knotted lace has been used to create a fantasy Mohican style. The natural hair at the sides has been coloured and blended into the false hair

Period hairdressing

There are techniques and equipment to help you create period hairstyles. Researching the period is necessary and fun. There are books, libraries and museums to help.

The style may be created using the artist's own hair or with wigs. Using the artist's hair eliminates the problems of disguising hair lace, but natural hair is fine and silky and sometimes difficult to secure. Another difficulty is achieving the height often required. However, there are hairpieces and crêpe hair that can be used to do that.

Design the style and plan what needs to be done to achieve it. If it is complicated, section off the hair and secure with large hair clips, and dress each section separately. If the style requires the back section to be 'put up', i.e. gripped up off the neck onto the crown, do this first by making large pincurls on the crown. Crossed hairgrips will give a more secure base onto which the hairpiece can be attached with large hairpins. The front and side section can then be dressed.

Attaching hairpieces

If the style requires ringlets or coils, a hairpiece can be added, leaving the front section of the natural hair to be dressed over the base. Hairpieces can be dressed beforehand or secured to the head and then dressed.

To attach the piece, make a pincurl and cross two hairgrips. Attach the base of the hairpiece to the curl with a hairpin, tucking the pin under the grips.

The back is put up first, making pincurls on the crown of the head. The hairpiece is attached. The sides are left to last to dress into the hairpiece

Backcombing

Backcombing the hair is helpful when dressing period styles as it gives more body to the hair.

- Take a section of hair and comb up from the roots;
- underneath the section, comb some hair back down towards the roots. This will hold the hair away from the head; smooth over the top of the hair so that the backcombing doesn't show;
- smooth over the top hair to cover the backcombing.

Comb some hair back towards the roots to make the hair stand away from the scalp

Making a French pleat

1. Comb the back hair to one side. The hair can be given extra body and control with some backcombing first

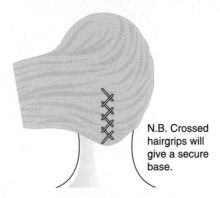

N.B. Crossed hairgrips will give a secure base.

2. Secure with hairgrips. Crossed hairgrips will give a secure base

3. Comb the hair back and tuck it into a roll

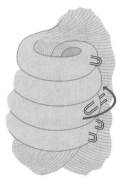

Take hairpin
through roll,
tuck under
and back
underneath
hairgrips.

4. Take hairpin through roll, tuck under and back underneath hairgrips

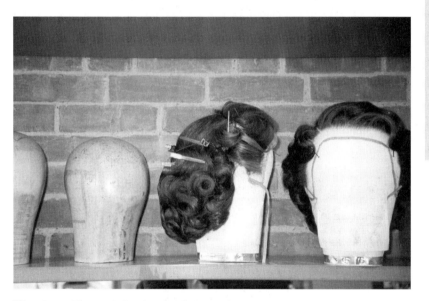

Wigs dressed in a period style using finger waving

Finger waving

Waved hair was a style popular in the 1930s. Sometimes metal clamps were used to hold the waves in place as the hair dried. Today there are light alloy clips that are much more comfortable and friendly!

It is important to learn to do this properly. If only the top layer of hair is waved, when combed through the waves will drop down and the style will not be true to the period.

1. Wet the hair thoroughly and comb straight, right through to the roots, with a parting at one side.
2. Starting at the top of the head by the parting, start the wave by combing the hair away from the face.
3. Hold the direction firmly with the second finger of the other hand.
4. Comb the hair round in the other direction creating a semi-circle. Make sure all the hair to the scalp has been combed.
5. Hold the new direction with the forefinger together with the middle finger, while combing the hair back towards the face.
6. With these fingers, 'pinch' the crest of the wave while combing the hair into the new wave.
7. Put the middle finger now on the new wave and, together with the forefinger, create a new crest by combing the hair back to the rear of the head again.
8. Keep combing the hair through to the roots at each wave and continue the waves to the ears.
9. Use clips to hold the waves securely and cover with a hair net to dry.
10. Finish the ends of the waves with pincurls in the correct direction.

Waves can be created by using reverse pincurls, i.e. one row of curls going clockwise and the next row going counter-clockwise. This method, however, will not produce such firm waving.

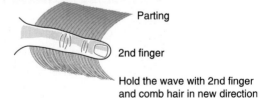

Parting

2nd finger

Hold the wave with 2nd finger and comb hair in new direction

Start the wave

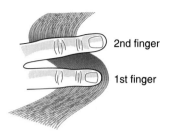

2nd finger

1st finger

Pinch 1st and 2nd fingers together to make a crest

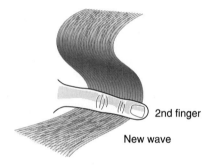

2nd finger

New wave

Move fingers down to continue the wave

The completed style

Marcel tongs and waving

Using Marcel tongs requires training and practice, but once mastered they do give a very strong and lasting set to the style. They are used on dry hair so are most valuable for redressing hair when the set is losing its curl.

There are different sizes of tongs, each giving a different amount of curl. The smallest tongs are mostly used for dressing facial hair, while the largest are used for waving. The tongs are heated in special heaters and it is important to judge the temperature well so that the hair is not burnt. If there is any doubt, the tongs can be tested on a piece of tissue.

Heat the tongs to the required temperature. Keep reheating them throughout the process to maintain this temperature.

1. With a tail comb, take a section of hair about two inches wide and one-quarter inch thick. Hold between the first two fingers of the left hand, or the right hand if you are left-handed. (For holding tongs see Dressing facial hair on page 112.)
2. Place the heated tongs at the roots of the hair, with the larger, lower jaw of the tongs facing upwards (see diagram 1).
3. Decide which way the wave is going and turn the tongs away from you, creating a crest (see diagram 2).
4. Slide the fingers of the other hand down the section of hair a little, encouraging it to create the wave. The heat of the tongs will 'set' the crest.
5. Holding the hair firmly in the 'free' hand, lift the tongs 'over' the crest and place back in the hair 'under' the crest (see diagram 3).
6. Turn the tongs towards you to create a crest going the opposite way to the previous one. Hold firmly with the tongs to strengthen the crest (see diagram 4).

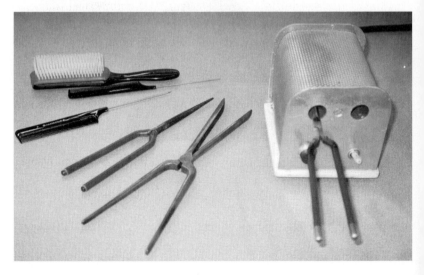

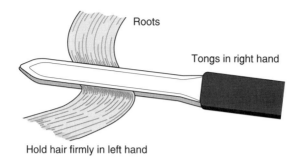

Roots

Tongs in right hand

Hold hair firmly in left hand

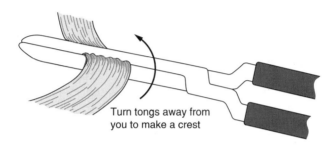

Turn tongs away from you to make a crest

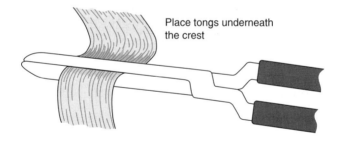

Place tongs underneath the crest

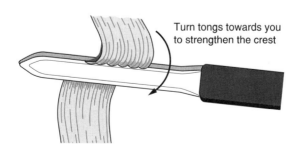

Turn tongs towards you to strengthen the crest

7. Slide the fingers of the other hand down through the hair again, encouraging the wave to go the other way.
8. Slide the tongs down the hair for two inches, or the width of the wave required, opening and closing the tongs quickly to heat the hair and reinforce the wave.
9. Work the tongs as before to make a new crest.

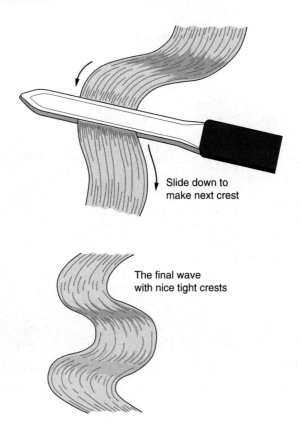

Slide down to
make next crest

The final wave
with nice tight crests

It will take a great deal of skill to complete a whole head of hair with this method so it is more commonly used for strengthening the waves of finger waving.

Curls and ringlets

- Pick up a small section of hair. If there is too much hair, the heat will not penetrate right through and the curl will not be very tight.
- Slide the tongs through the hair to the ends and hold the hair in the tongs.
- Roll the tongs, holding the hair, up to the roots, curling the hair around the tongs.
- Hold in position until the tongs have cooled and then release. The hair should fall into ringlets.

The tongs can be placed in the hair at the roots and the hair wound around them. This will give curls but they will not be as tight as those made by the above method.

Ringlets are more often 'wet set' using wooden sticks. Even rolled up newspaper can be used to good effect

Wigs and hairpieces

Wigs

Wigs vary a great deal in price and quality. There are some very good machine-produced wigs available now at reasonable prices. They are made with stretchable foundations to fit all sizes of head. Some are made from real hair and some from synthetic hair; it is important to remember that the camera reacts differently to synthetic materials. Natural hair absorbs the light better and is, in fact, made up of very many colours. Nylon is very shiny and will catch the light. A synthetic wig is likely to be dyed all one colour, giving a very dense, false effect on camera. This does not mean that it cannot be used, but these points should be considered, especially if the work is with studio lighting.

For wigs made with real hair, there are suppliers who fit, make and dress wigs, not only for television, cinema and theatre but also for members of the public. They carry a stock of wigs and other postiches, such as switches, pincurls, toupees and backfalls. All are available to hire or buy, but if the wig needs to fit well, that is for a member of the public or if an artist is to be seen in close-up, the wig may need to be specially made and fitted. If a make-up designer or hairdresser is working on a large production requiring many wigs, most will be hired. However, if the wig is being used for any length of time it may be cheaper to buy it.

It is not always necessary to have a full wig. Hard fronted wigs, i.e. with no lace foundation at the front, are made to fit the back of the head, using the natural hair around the hairline to cover the wig front. This reduces the problem of disguising the hair lace, but the hair has to be matched accurately to the artist's own as a camera will pick out easily a change in hair colour.

If a wig is a good fit but the hair lace is not in good condition, it can be refronted, i.e. the whole front section of the wig can be renewed with fine lace. There are wigs made entirely on hair lace. These are very expensive and very delicate. They would probably be used over a bald cap to give the effect of balding or very thin hair.

Toupees

Toupees, or hairpieces for men, are knotted completely on fine hair lace, as they need to be secured carefully to the head, usually with double-sided tape or glue, and small clips or wig springs to attach the piece to any hair. These also need to be carefully matched with the colour of the natural hair that will be brushed into them to disguise the hairpiece.

A hairlace wig and a wig knotted on large-holed netting

A toupee with a hairlace foundation

Hairpieces

There are also hairpieces, or postiche, made for adding to wigs. These are used mostly to create period hairstyles, for instance ringlets or the huge curls that were popular in the 1960s. These are made by weaving the hair onto thread and sewing into different shapes of postiche.

The wefts can also be twisted into a 'switch' or a smaller 'pincurl' with a loop for attaching. A switch can be plaited or coiled or dressed into ringlets.

Making a switch or a pincurl is illustrated below.

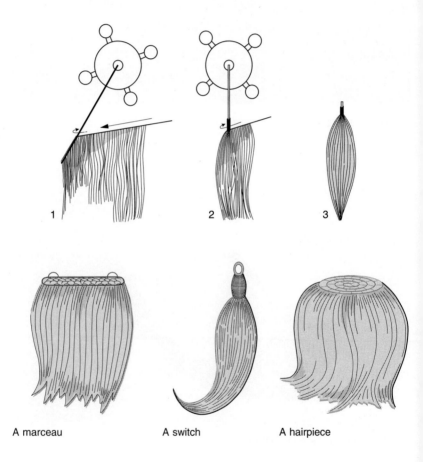

A marceau   A switch   A hairpiece

Weaving

This makes a long weft of hair that is either folded and sewn into straight sections of hair or marteau, used for making waves, or is made into a round hairpiece or chignon that is used for adding fullness or dressing to curls and other period styles.

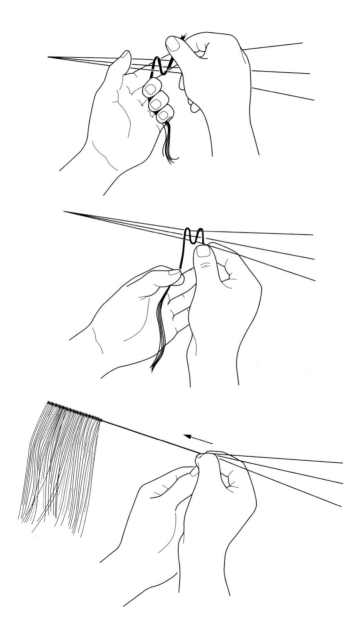

The making of wigs

The cap or base of a wig is called the wig foundation and onto this the hair is knotted, if it is a man-made wig, or sewn, if it is machine made. Around the circumference of the wig the foundation must be firm and fitted with more accuracy. This is mainly where the wig will be anchored with grips to the head, although there may be some grips used on the crown.

For media work man-made, natural hair wigs are mostly used. Wooden blocks are used to make the foundations, and these come in different sizes. Measurements are taken of the head, and a block of the appropriate size is marked out. Hair lace is then pinned to the block, tucking and pleating where appropriate to fit. Small bones are used to shape the front and sides of the hairline to give shape and strength to the wig.

Hair lace is available in different thicknesses. For the large area over the crown large-holed netting called caul net is used instead of lace. Around the edges, particularly around the front hairline, a finer hair lace is used. This is designed to be glued onto the forehead and to disappear into the skin. If the wig is being used for theatre the hair lace can be stronger, but for film or TV, where it is important that the hair lace must not be at all noticeable, it has to very fine indeed.

When the foundation is completed the hair is knotted onto the lace. Knotting is done with knotting hooks that, again, come in various sizes depending on the fineness of the lace being used. Knotting is explained on page 142. When the wig is completed the hair can then be cut and taken off the block ready for fitting and dressing.

A wig room

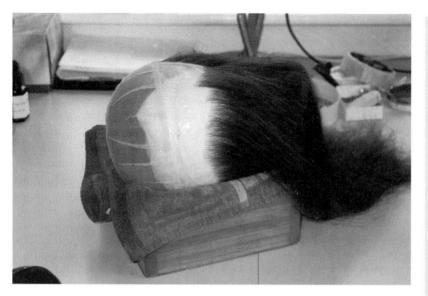

The block rests in a block holder while it is being knotted

Each hair is carefully knotted onto the lace. It is painstaking work

141

Knotting

Knotting is done with knotting hooks of various sizes, the size dictated by the fineness of the lace being knotted. At the front of the wig only two or three hairs will be picked up to be knotted. A larger hook will pick up six or seven hairs to be knotted on the crown and back sections.

A small amount of hair at the root end is held between the finger and thumb, turning the roots over in a small loop. One or two hairs are picked up by the knotting hook and anchored onto the lace.

The hair will lie in the direction of the knot so it is important that the lace is knotted in the direction that the hair grows naturally.

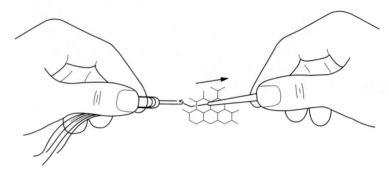

The knotting hook picks up one or two hairs

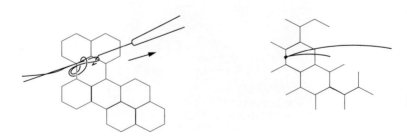

The hair is pulled through the lace and knotted through itself

The knot secured

Taking the measurements of a head

For wigs to look and move like real hair they have to fit accurately, especially around the hairline and around the nape of the neck. If the wig is too large there will be too much hair to dress and if too small it is likely that the hair will not sit properly onto the neck.

When taking measurements to pass on to a wigmaker there are specific measurements required.

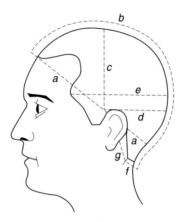

Measurements of the head required: a, circumference; b, from centre forehead to nape over crown; c, from ear to ear over crown; d, from ear to ear around back; e, from temple to temple around back; f, across nape; g, from ear across nape

It is also important to take note of the natural hairline and a pattern may have to be made.

Taking an impression of the head

If it is not possible for an artist to attend a wig fitting there is an extremely satisfactory way to measure their head using clingfilm. The hair is flattened down to the head as close as possible, either in large flat pincurls, or by wrapping the hair and pinning. If the hair is not too long there are products available that will flatten the hair to the head, but it is important to be able to see the back hairline.

Place clingfilm all over the head and ask the artist to hold it firmly. Cover the clingfilm with strips of clear sticky tape all over the head. This will give strength to the clingfilm. Once completely covered and firm, with an indelible marker pen draw around the hairline as accurately as possible. This 'cap' can now be lifted off the hair and will give an accurate shape of the head.

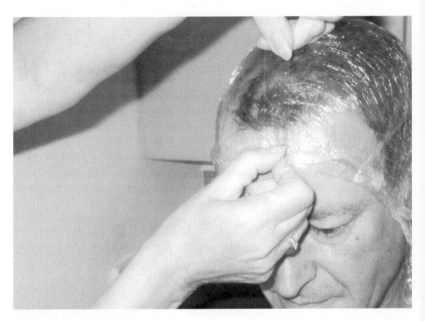

Taking an impression of a head

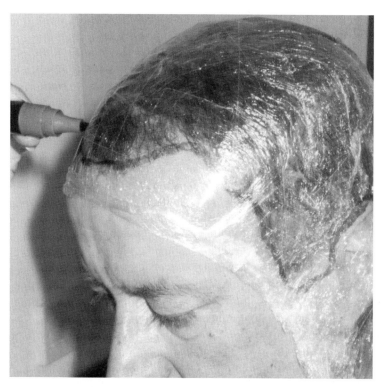

The hairline is marked out on the clingfilm impression

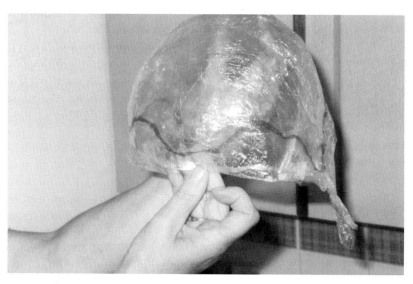

The cap can be cut to size

Blocking a wig

It is extremely important to block a wig, i.e. secure it on a specially shaped block, whenever it is not being used. To do this, a malleable block is used, which is a firm block filled with sawdust and covered in cotton. Blocks are available in various sizes to suit different wig sizes. It is important that the hair lace is not stretched.

The block keeps the shape of the wig but also protects the wig and hair lace while the wig is being dressed. The wig is placed on the block, making sure that it is sitting straight and lies neatly. Large 'T' pins are used to secure it around the back and the ears. Blocking tape, sometimes known as galloon, is pinned onto the lace with very small pins. Two rows of pins are used to spread the pull on the lace if it is fine lace, as used for television.

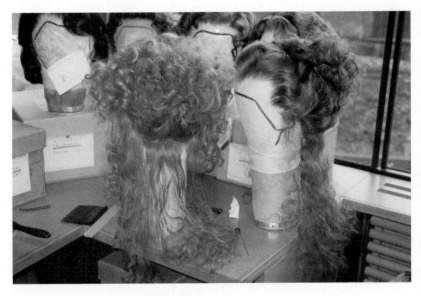

Note the extra long neck on the wig block

Dressing wigs

The hair on wigs and hairpieces will have been chemically treated and therefore will not have the same 'life' that natural hair has. It will have been straightened and pre-curled and will be, generally, easier to dress. However, it will need a firmer dressing as it will not have the lift that natural hair has.

Period hairstyles can be very complicated and it is helpful to have a systematic way of working. First, the hair is brushed through completely and divided into four sections: the top, the two sides and the back. Any hairpieces required will be attached next so that the side and front hair will cover the base. It is easier if the style is dressed from underneath up to the top and front.

The back section is dressed first, especially if it is to be dressed up off the neck, as in a French pleat, then the side sections and finally the front. Other than the flat-waved era of the 1920s, period hairstyles tend to be quite big and full. Crêpe hair can be used to give extra fullness, along with backcombing the hair. Backcombing the hair will also give more control over the hair while creating the style.

Wigs are usually sprayed quite heavily with hair lacquer to keep their shape as they will need to be packed in boxes for transportation and storage.

Applying wigs

For the wig to look 'natural' the hair underneath must be as flat as possible. If the artist's hair is short it need only be flattened with water or gel. If it is long it needs to be flattened by wrapping the hair flat to the head and securing with grips, or set and held in large flat pincurls.

Points to remember:

- crossed pincurls on the crown of the head underneath the wig will give points for securing the wig to the head with large hairpins;
- always put the wig on from the front of the head, matching the natural hairline as much as possible. Ask the artist to hold down the front of the wig – not the hair lace – while you pull it over the crown;
- using the mirror, make sure the wig is sitting straight and is comfortable around the ears;
- secure the wig above the ears with hairgrips;
- stick the hair lace using as little spirit gum as possible – it may only need to be stuck in one or two places. Hair lace is delicate and can only be used and cleaned a finite number of times. It also stretches easily so must be handled as little as possible. Wherever possible a sable brush must be used for sticking and cleaning it to preserve its lifespan;
- secure the wig with grips at other points, such as behind the ears, either side of the nape of the neck and through the pincurls under the wig. Check with the artist that the pins and grips are comfortable. After a while they can pull or stick into the head and be quite painful;
- take care when doing any final dressing that the wig is not pulled too much. This may cause the wig to dislodge or be uncomfortable for the artist.

Applying hard-fronted wigs

The wig may not have a hair lace front and be designed to be used with the artist's own hair. Section off the artist's hair from ear to ear around the front hairline. Attach the wig behind this section with grips. Dress the natural hair back and into the dressed wig. It is likely that some hairspray will be needed to keep the natural hair secure.

Sticking hair lace

Spirit gum is used for sticking hair lace. It is a natural product that comes from gum trees. There are several gums to choose from, depending on what is required. A thick gum will stick firmly, but it may possibly shine. Thicker gum could be useful in theatre work but for TV or film work a finer gum may have to be used. It is possible to get matt gum.

Paint the gum onto the skin and wait a few seconds for it to become tacky. Apply the lace and press firmly with a damp cloth. The cloth will prevent the gum from sticking to fingers and will keep the lace clean.

It may not be necessary to glue all around the hairline. If the wig front is of fine lace and a good fit, the hair lace should seem to disappear into the skin. If the wig is well secured, it may only be necessary to catch the lace with glue in the centre of the forehead and from the temples down in front of the ears. The less gum that is used, the less likely it is to catch the light. If the hair lace moves a lot it may pick up some foundation and will need to be cleaned. This can be done once the wig is removed by placing a tissue under the lace and brushing the lace gently with some surgical spirit.

When removing the wig, remove any spirit gum with a small sable brush, tucking the brush under the lace gently to lift it from the skin. Take out the grips and pins used to secure it and, holding the wig on each side above and behind the ears, lift it forwards over the top of the head towards the face. Place on a malleable block.

Powdered wigs have a hard front as they are meant to look false

Maintaining and cleaning wigs and hairpieces

After removal of a wig, the hair lace needs to be cleaned. Surgical spirit is used to lift the hair lace from the artist's face, but acetone or methylated spirit are also good for cleaning stubborn gum or dirt left on the lace.

- Place the hair lace onto a clean towel, cloth or tissue.
- Use a glass or metal bowl for the spirit.
- Use a toothbrush or similar hard-bristled brush.
- Tap the lace with the spirit-soaked brush. The gum and dirt will soak into the cloth or paper.
- Do not rub. Hair lace is delicate and will damage easily.
- If the lace is badly soiled, it can be soaked in acetone or methylated spirit for a while.
- Work in a well-ventilated room.

Cleaning wigs
When a wig has been dressed by a wig specialist it will have a firm set so that it will hold its shape for some time. The re-dressing, therefore, may only be re-combing and smoothing out the original dressing. Sometimes, however, it may require some major re-dressing. The wig generally won't be cleaned until it is no longer needed for the production.

Shampoo can be used for cleaning synthetic hair. The wigs and pieces should be cleaned gently in a bowl of warm, soapy water. Dip, using an up and down movement, taking care not to tangle the hair. After rinsing they can be patted dry in a towel and blocked. They can be wet set or dried first and then dressed with tongs or heated rollers.

If hair is cleaned with recommended dry cleaning solvents, this must be done with great care.

- It must *always* be done in a well-ventilated room, as the fumes are toxic.
- Always use glass or metal bowls. The solvent will melt plastic.
- Gently move the hair in the fluid. Do not scrub, the solvent will lift the dirt.
- Lift out and drain the excess fluid back into the bowl.
- Gently shake the wig and hang up to allow the fluid to evaporate.

When a wig has been cleaned place it on a malleable block to keep it clean and hold its shape.

Introduction to special effects

Creating special effects is one of the most exciting aspects of working as a make-up artist. The sense of achievement in having produced realistic effects is tremendous. As always, the secret of success is that the special effects do not look like make-up. This means that subtlety is required; little rather than more make-up will give best results. Experiment with tools for application – stipple sponges, hairpins, the end of a brush rather than the bristle, and a variety of modelling tools.

- Research is paramount not only for accurate coloration but to establish where the make-up should be applied. If someone has fallen and bruised his or her face, the bruise would more likely be on a prominent bone, cheekbone or forehead for instance, not on a soft area.
- Continuity must be considered and planned for. A bruise or wound doesn't suddenly vanish overnight and the healing process needs to be considered.
- It is worthwhile checking, if possible, how it will be filmed. A lot of work could be done only to find that it was on the wrong side of the face or body! The amount of make-up required would be affected by whether it is to be filmed as a long shot or a close-up.

Bruising

Dirt or breaking down

'Breaking down' is the term used for creating the effects required when an artist is affected by environmental conditions in the story. It can be just making someone look hot and sweaty or showing that they have been in a dirty place. Again it is important that these effects look realistic.

The make-up artist needs to ask the following questions:

- How did the person get dirty?
- If a child has dirty hands and rubs his or her face, where would the dirt be?
- If a person were perspiring, where would it show most?
- If someone were crying, how would the tears fall?

There are many products now made especially for TV and film – coloured powders, coloured gels, specially coloured grease paints. There's even tooth enamel that gives the appearance of rotting teeth.

It is surprising, though, what can be found in the kitchen cupboard that will do just as well as commercial products. Sometimes mixing your own colours and materials produces more realistic effects than manufactured products. However, don't get carried away. Vegetable soup is wonderful as fake vomit, but looks so awful the audience may end up feeling sick!

Although food products should be safe to use, if in doubt test the products on a sensitive area of skin such as behind the ears or on the inside of the wrist, and use a barrier cream.

Tears and sweat

Tear sticks, available to buy, are held near the eyes to make them water; there are also such products as Epsom Salts and Olbas Oil that have the same effect. However, care must be taken when using them. Some people have extremely sensitive eyes. Eye drops used in excess may give just as good an effect.

Glycerine is an extremely useful product to have. By dropping a little under the eyes it will trickle slowly creating the effect of tears. It can also be stippled onto the face and body to give the effect of sweat. It does not dry out as quickly as water. Be very careful not to get glycerine in the eyes as it can sting for some time. Make sure that it is cleaned off the face before the artist rubs their eyes.

A mixture of glycerine and water is effective as sweat and can be kept in a small water spray for speed of application. It is shiny and catches the light. It does not dry up like pure water. Pure glycerine will give heavy globules, but again make sure the products are cleaned off the skin when filming is finished.

Blood

The colour of blood should not be taken for granted. It needs thought and research. Arterial blood is brighter than venous blood because it is oxygenated and congealed blood turns darker the longer it is left. Blood can be bought ready-made in both light and dark colours but consideration must be given to staining; some blood products will stain both skin and clothes. It is important for costume staff to check with make-up about staining if blood is being used.

To make your own, commercial blood can be mixed with water and red and yellow food colouring. The thickness can be varied by adding flour or glycerine or clear syrup to make it more viscous. Adding black treacle, more flour or crushed breadcrumbs will create congealed blood. Adding crushed cereals will create various bloody wounds and grazes.

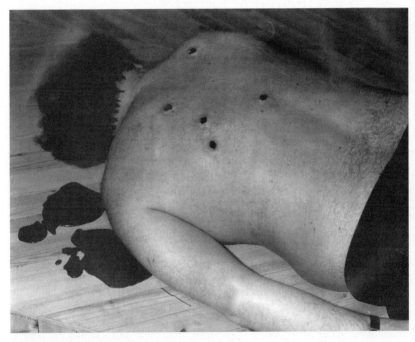

For authenticity all wounds need to be researched. If someone is shot, the entry wound caused by the bullet will be small, the greater damage being internally or at the point where the bullet exits. These bullet wounds were made from wax straight onto the skin

When working with blood and wounds continuity has to be carefully researched and noted. As the days pass the wound needs to be in the right place and as it heals any bruising will change colour.

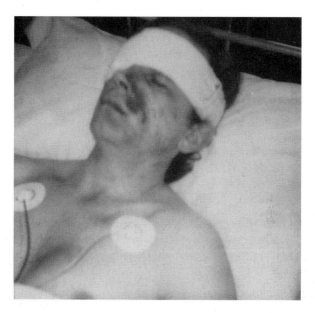

Planning the wounds beforehand is important for continuity

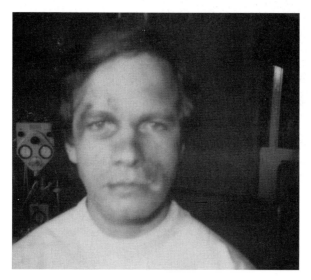

As the wounds heal the make-up must be consistent, which is not always straightforward if the scenes are shot out of sequence. These grazes were created with latex

Latex

Latex, another versatile material, can be used straight from the tube for working directly onto skin or it can be moulded and used in prosthetics. Surgical adhesive, like that usually used for sticking false eyelashes, can also be used for small scars. Latex and similar plastic materials are quick and easy to use.

Making a wound or a scar on skin
Small wounds and scars can be made directly onto the skin:

- rub some barrier cream into the skin;
- mark the wound or scar with an eye or lip pencil;
- apply latex or plastic to the area from the tube or with a modelling tool;
- smooth the edges into the skin and model it as it dries;
- apply make-up as necessary and powder. The latex will look smooth and shiny, as does a scar;
- if the required effect is a new wound, additions such as tissue, cotton wool and blood effects can be added to the drying latex. Even stitches can be added by tying knots in dark, thick cotton, cutting the thread either side and placing them in the latex;
- the skin can be made to appear as if it is peeling by lifting the edges of the latex. Blisters can be made by making a hole in the latex and lifting it to form a bubble;
- cornflakes and other breakfast cereals make excellent scabs and grazes.

Latex is also used for manufacturing pieces such as bald caps. The latex is painted onto a plastic block, allowed to dry and built up in layers, leaving the outside edges very fine to blend into the skin. False noses and scars can also be bought ready made. They are available in various sizes and shapes and are applied with spirit gum. Some are fine enough to be used for TV and film, certainly for background shots, but many are too big and heavy and are only suitable for theatre work. It is better to make your own.

Making scars and wounds in latex or plastic
Small pieces such as scars and burns can be made by painting latex or plastic straight into a negative mould. The mould is made from a scar or wound that has been modelled on a flat board.

- To make your own mould, model the scar or wound in clay or plasticine.
- When dry, brush the whole with petroleum jelly or sugar soap, which will act as a separating agent.

- Cover the model with plaster of Paris or dental stone to a thickness of about one and a half inches to make a negative mould.
- When dry remove the mould from the model.
- Seal the inside of the mould with shellac.
- When completely dry, the latex or plastic can be brushed into the mould to the thickness desired. Colour can be added to the latex by scraping pancake, or pressed powder base, into the liquid. Build up the layers but leave the edges thin for blending into the skin.
- Use talcum powder and a soft brush to lift out the latex piece from the mould. Talcum the piece all over as you proceed to stop it sticking to itself.

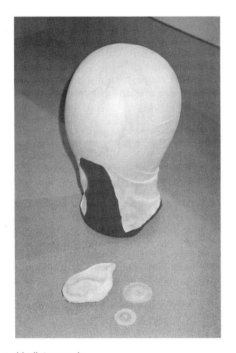

A bald cap, ears and bullet wounds

Mortician's wax

This is one of the oldest materials used in creating make-up effects. It is available in two consistencies, soft and hard. The soft wax softens easily with the heat from hands or skin so is more pliable and possibly easier to mould. However, it can become sticky if over-worked and some people prefer working with the harder wax after it is warmed. Wax is best applied and moulded with a tool such as a palette knife or modelling tool so that it can be moulded without 'dragging' and finely blended away into the skin to disguise the edges. A little cream or moisturiser on the finger will smooth it out and help blending.

Wax is very versatile:

- it can change the shape of noses, chins and ears;
- it can become warts, cuts and grazes;
- it can also be used to block out eyebrows, i.e. to flatten them so that they can be painted over as though they are not there, as in clown make-up;
- it can be textured, i.e. given a skin-like appearance by gently pressing a cloth or sponge onto the surface.

Building a false nose with wax

It is crucial that you work looking in the mirror. The wax must be modelled to the shape of the face from all angles and the mirror will show you whether there are any telltale bumps that need to be blended away.

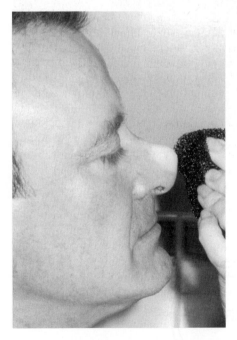

Texture is added to the wax with a stipple sponge

When satisfactory modelling is complete, it must be sealed. There is a preparative sealer for this, which is painted on with a brush. When the sealer is dry, add a second coat and a little powder to take away some of the shine. Isopropyl alcohol will clean the brushes.

The danger with wax is that it remains pliable and so if knocked can be easily cut or dented. On the other hand, it can be easily repaired. Its versatility makes it an invaluable part of a make-up artist's kit.

Blocking out eyebrows

For some characters it is necessary to 'remove' the eyebrows, for example for clown make-up, or for an Elizabethan make-up to reflect the fashion of the time for shaving off the eyebrows and drawing them on with pencil.

Soap can be used just as well as wax. Soak a corner of the soap in warm water until it is soft. Apply the soft soap with a pallet knife. When it is dry it can be made-up.

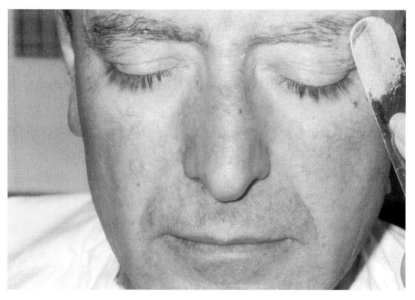

Blocking out eyebrows. The wax is applied with a flat tool and pressed in to the hairs. When the hair is flat and the wax smooth with no 'edges' the area can be sealed and made-up

Gelatine

There are products such as congealed blood and blushing gel that are useful to keep in your kit, but they are sold in small quantities and are expensive to use on a large scale.

Gelatine is a very good alternative substance for making wounds and accident effects. Prosthetic pieces can also be made from it. It can be melted and coloured in advance and then carried around in its solid form. It is largely harmless and is simply washed off with soap and water.

Once melted, it is so quick and effective that it is particularly useful for such things as making-up crowd artists involved in a multiple crash.

- Put some gelatine, glycerine and a small quantity of water in a pan.
- Heat until the gelatine has melted.
- Add more water if a softer jelly is required. It can be tested by putting some mixture onto a cold surface to cool and set.
- Add colouring – make-up or food colouring.
- When it is a comfortable temperature, dip a brush or sponge into the mixture and apply to the skin. It cools quickly and, depending on the thickness, will either set or stay soft and pliable.
- As with latex, anything can be added to the mixture while it is setting, e.g. dirt, crushed cornflakes.
- The 'skin' can be broken and dripping blood can be added.

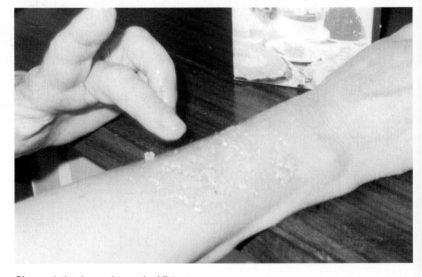

Clear gelatine is used to make blisters

Introduction to prosthetics

Anything fitted to a person's face or body, other than hair, is called a prosthesis. A prosthesis can be made out of gelatine, latex, plastic, rubber or foam. There are several reasons why a prosthesis may be needed:

1. to change the shape of the face or body;
2. for speed of application;
3. if there is time to research and plan wounds, such as major burns, a better result is achieved by making them in advance;
4. it may be that a particular effect is needed for scenes shot over several days, in which case several pieces can be made at the same time to facilitate continuity.

False noses and other prosthetic pieces

When a prosthesis is used to change the shape of a face, or part of a face, an accurate impression must be taken so that the piece will fit exactly. A face cast is needed from which two moulds are made: a positive and a negative.

The 'new' face is then modelled on the positive, a negative mould taken of the modelling, and the prosthesis is made by filling the space between the two moulds with the appropriate material: latex, gelatine or foam.

'A Tale of Pig Robinson'. A Dreamscape Production, filmed by TVS

Modelling

For making small prostheses, use a plaster of Paris or plastic mould of a face or body part to model the wound, scar or other prosthesis in plasticine or modelling material. Good quality clay can also be used but it must be kept very damp. Keep the clay tightly enclosed in a polythene or plastic bag until the modelling is completed. The modelling should also be left covered with a damp cloth so that it doesn't dry out. Once finished, it can be left to air dry. Plasterline is a very good oil-based modelling material that does not need to dry out. However, some people do not find it so easy to work with.

Modelling tools vary in quality and come in different shapes and sizes. The best tools for this work are metal dentistry tools as the modelling needs to be precise. Modelling skills need to be perfected in order to achieve realistic results.

If the prosthesis is to be made between two moulds, there must be a means for excess material to escape. This is achieved by forming a channel round the modelling with exit points. A coil of material, about one-quarter of an inch thick, is placed all round the modelling about half an inch from the edge with short coils branching off to the edge of the mould. When the second mould is made it will then have channels with exit points to allow excess material to drain off.

Modelling noses of various shapes

Working with plaster or stone

Plaster of Paris is a good material with which to make moulds and is easy to use, though it can be heavy if too much is used. It produces a soft 'stone' so is easily damaged. Dental stone gives a harder result so the lifespan of impressions is longer. Very large moulds can be strengthened by adding hessian, scrim or fine garden mesh to the final layers.

It is extremely important to realize that you must know what you are doing and be proficient at working with these materials *before* attempting to take an impression of someone's face. Plaster is *never* applied directly to skin. The impression is taken first with Alginate, a dental material, and the plaster used over that to give it strength.

Plaster will stick to plaster, so it is important to seal every mould with shellac, sugar soap or petroleum jelly so that the moulds will separate.

1. Pour some water into a large mixing bowl and add the plaster. Allow the plaster to soak into the water. It is better to add too little than too much at first.
2. Mix the two together gently with your hands. This is so that you can feel the plaster 'going off'. Tap the bowl to bring air bubbles to the surface. Trapped air bubbles will lead to imperfect casts.
3. When mixing plaster or dental stone there comes a point when it starts to 'go off' or set. It begins to warm up, to feel creamy and starts to thicken. This is the point when it is applied to the Alginate or modelling. It sets very quickly. Once set it cannot be manipulated, so it is better to mix small quantities because fresh plaster can be added to setting plaster. Practice is required.
4. When making a negative mould, drip the plaster over the modelling first and then build up. It needs to be substantial, but anything much over one-inch thick and it will become too heavy. The top should be flat so that it will sit firmly on a bench to be worked on.
5. The plaster will cool down as it sets. When dry, it can be lifted from the modelling and the positive mould. Inside you will see the negative of the modelling.
6. Seal the plaster with shellac, sugar soap or petroleum jelly.

Plaster bandage
Plaster bandage is bandage impregnated with plaster. A piece of bandage is cut and dipped into water. Excess water is drained off and the bandage placed in position. As it dries it holds its shape. It is often used as a final layer to Alginate or a mould to give it strength.

Life casts of face or body

A great deal of skill is required for the materials used in this work. The materials have 'setting' times and the work has to be done quickly, efficiently and safely. It is essential to practise thoroughly on hands or other parts of the body before attempting the face.

To take a face cast it is crucial to know what you're doing. All but the nostrils are covered, which could be claustrophobic for the subject. You must have experience of having a face cast done of yourself, so that you know what it feels like at each stage. This will help you talk through and reassure the artist undergoing the cast. Confidence and a calm atmosphere throughout are essential. It is best to have someone else with you, preferably a nurse or someone trained in first aid.

Alginate

Alginate is used in dentistry to take impressions of the teeth. It is harmless and not unpleasant to smell or taste. It is mixed with water, which is usually cold as warm water speeds up the setting process. It still sets quickly, however, in about three minutes. It sets into a firm jelly but needs support to keep its shape and will shrink in time. Consequently, the positive mould must be made as soon as the cast is taken.

To take a face cast:

1. Make sure the artist is comfortable, relaxed and all clothes protected with a gown and towels. He or she should know in detail what is going to be done and be clear that the materials will be removed at any point if necessary.
2. Protect hair with a cap and apply petroleum jelly or grease to any facial hair to prevent it sticking to the Alginate.
3. The artist should be seated in an upright position looking ahead to give an accurate impression.
4. Mix the Alginate as per manufacturer's instructions, taking care not to over-agitate and create air bubbles.
5. Apply the Alginate to the face starting at the forehead, leaving the nose and mouth to last. It will feel cold at first but will warm up. Use your hands to 'drop' the Alginate onto the skin.
6. Take care to ensure that the skin is covered and no air is trapped, particularly in the corners of the nose.
7. Leave the nostrils free and an airway through the mouth using a tube or straw.
8. Apply an even layer of Alginate and, when set, reinforce with plaster or plaster bandage. Make sure the edges are well supported ready for removal.
9. When the plaster has set, gently lift the edges of the cast from the face.
10. If the artist bends forwards and moves his or her face, the Alginate should come away from the face more easily.
11. Clean the face with damp cotton wool. Tone and moisturize the skin.

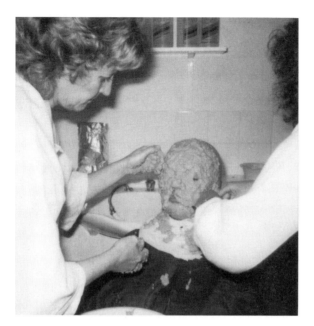

Leave nose and mouth until last

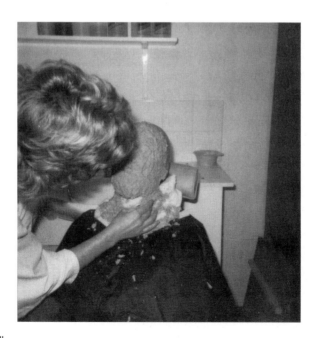

Cover well

Life casts of face or body

165

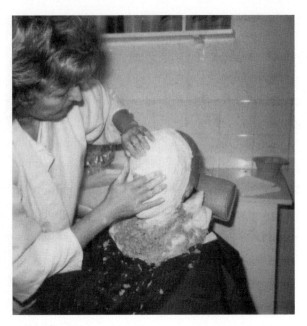

Apply plaster to support Alginate

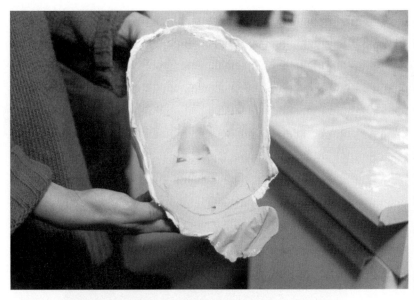

The Alginate, supported by plaster, is removed from the face. What can be seen is the 'negative' impression of the face, i.e. the 'inside' of the face

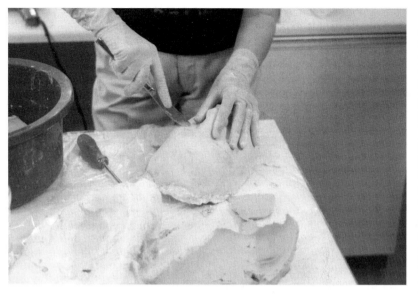

Any holes having been filled, the Alginate mould is filled with plaster or stone to create the 'positive' impression, onto which the alterations to the face will be modelled

Making a positive mould

1. Fill any holes in the Alginate cast, such as nostrils and mouth.
2. Mix a bowl of plaster.
3. Paint in a layer of plaster, making sure there are no air bubbles.
4. Build up the mould with layers of plaster to about one and a half inches and allow to dry thoroughly.
5. Peel off the Alginate and clean the mould.
6. Put the positive face cast on a board rubbed with petroleum jelly, ready to set it in a plaster base.
7. Build a frame round the board using wooden slats.
8. Raise the cast an inch or two with clay and fill the frame with plaster, encasing the edge of the cast.
9. When set, remove the slats. You should have a good smooth mould to work with.
10. With a drill, make two or three dents or chips in the plaster base to ensure accurate fitting of the moulds when they are put together.
11. Seal the plaster with shellac or sugar soap.

Clay is used to hold the frame in place, and straw or hessian used to give extra strength to the plaster base.

Build a frame

Plaster base for the mould. The positive mould ready for sealing and modelling

Modelling

Making a negative mould

1. Having completed the modelling on the positive mould, rub the whole mould with petroleum jelly.
2. Rebuild the frame around the mould with the wooden slats.
3. Mix the plaster and pour into the box to a thickness of two or three inches. Tap gently to ensure there are no air bubbles.
4. Build up the plaster over the positive mould and model.
5. Level off the top of the plaster so that the mould will sit firmly on a bench.
6. When the plaster is set, remove the slats and allow the plaster to dry thoroughly. This can take a day or more. If it is not sufficiently dry, it could break during separation.
7. Separate the moulds carefully. You will probably need to use a firm tool such as a large screwdriver.
8. Remove the modelling material and clean both moulds.
9. Seal with shellac.
10. When the two moulds are put together there will now be a 'space' which, when filled with an appropriate material, will form the prosthesis.

The frame is rebuilt and the negative impression of the model is built up. The top of the plaster is smoothed to make a stable base for standing on the bench

Modelling is completed on a positive mould and a negative impression taken

Piece moulds

If the character's face needs to move in a realistic way, it may be necessary to make many separate pieces to build up the whole face. Once the modelling has been designed, each section has to be made separately. Each section has to have fine edges to stick to the skin. This requires the making of several sectional moulds, each with a positive and a negative. It takes a great deal of time and money. Consequently, this work is usually undertaken by prosthetics specialists.

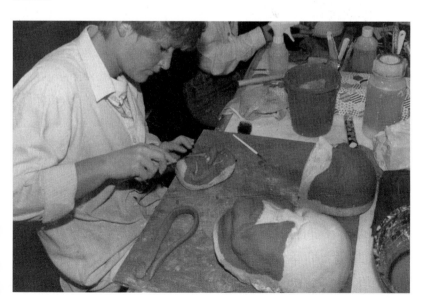

Foam latex pieces

The invention of foam latex pieces revolutionized make-up special effects. The matt surface does not reflect light in the same way as other materials; it is light to wear, making prolonged wear more comfortable; and it creates a more realistic appearance.

If an ageing make-up requires prosthetics there will be many very fine, small pieces made for each section of the face to enable the face to move naturally. Larger pieces would restrict this natural movement.

The making of these pieces is very specialized and is generally contracted out to people with the required scientific background. The make-up could be designed by the make-up designer for the production and then discussed and finalized with the prosthetics specialist.

However, small quantities of latex foam can be purchased. It is important to understand the principles of working with this material:

- the latex is treated with ammonia to thicken it;
- the foam agent is whisked in to produce the foam;
- the curing agent is a chemical mixture that changes its state when exposed to heat;
- the gelling agent solidifies the foam.

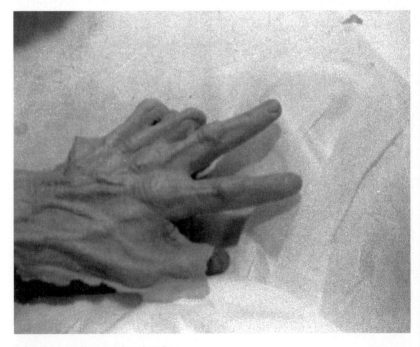

A foam latex piece used on hands

This is a chemical reaction that requires correct conditions, such as temperature, and accurate quantities. It requires experience to understand the difficulties.

It is very important to realize that, until the foam is cured in the oven, all these stages use *highly toxic* chemicals. It is dangerous to inhale the fumes at any time and masks *must* be worn. The work should be done in a well-ventilated room and with strict safety precautions observed at all times. All bottles should be well labelled and kept safe with the tops replaced securely immediately after use. Wear protective gloves and wash chemicals off skin and surfaces with cold water immediately.

Foam pieces can only be used once as the removal products melt the foam latex and the edges are ruined. This means that for every day that the make-up is required new pieces have to be used. That could mean the production of a lot of pieces! They also take a long time to apply and remove, which can add several hours to the usual working time. Artists should be considered at all times and be made aware of the difficulties involved in working in this way. There are many things to consider when planning this kind of work.

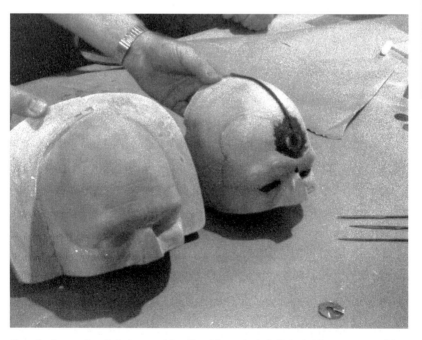

Here the foam piece is being used for disguising a technical device for some special effects

Application of prosthetic pieces

It is important to place the piece accurately on the face to ensure a good fit. Once the position is correct, it is helpful to mark it by dusting powder around the edge. Begin sticking the piece in the centre of the area and work outwards, sticking the fine edges last.

Different adhesives are used for different materials:

- spirit gum and medical adhesive such as Dow Corning 355 will stick latex, plastic and gelatine;
- there are manufactured products such as ProsAide to stick latex foam pieces.

To blend the edges:

- witch hazel can be used to blend the edges of gelatine pieces;
- if the piece is made of plastic, the edges can be melted with acetone;
- Duo, a surgical adhesive, can be used to cover the edges of latex and foam pieces.

Removal of prosthetic pieces

Pieces attached with spirit gum can be removed with manufactured products such as Mastix Remover or a spirit gum removal cream. Use a brush to lift the edges and work underneath the piece.

Isopropyl alcohol or an oil-based product such as Klene-All will remove pieces attached by medical adhesive.

Animal faces using two sections, the nose section and lower mouth section

Having fun

Whatever the materials used, character make-up provides the greatest challenge, the greatest satisfaction and, hopefully, the most fun.

Learning can be great fun!

A break in filming is enjoyed by all

Costume department

All costume personnel must have a pleasant easy-going personality, and be sensitive to others. They work with artists at a very personal level, who may be anxious or easily embarrassed, or may just have very strong ideas about themselves and how they look. It is important to be able to build up a good relationship with artists.

Clown

Costume assistant

The main priority for costume assistants, sometimes called dressers, is to provide clean, well-ironed clothes. The exception is for character reasons, when the clothes would need to be 'broken down', i.e. made dirty or blood-stained as the script necessitates. Maintenance of clothes is essential, regular laundering is necessary and repairs may also be needed.

If the production is a short presentation or interview the participants will wear their own clothes. They may or may not have received advice on what to wear. The costume assistant should check that their clothes do not need ironing and that they look tidy. It is likely that microphones will be pinned to their clothes and help with this may be necessary.

On a larger production or film the costume staff have to allocate and label the various costumes for the artists and make sure they are hanging carefully ready for use. Alongside make-up and hairdressing departments, costume personnel are usually the first members of the crew to arrive on set. Having been given the schedule for the day, the clothes required and the relevant artists, the clothes may be distributed to the various dressing rooms. Calls will be worked out with the artist and other departments as to when the assistant will be available to help. It may be that the artist will need to go to the costume department to dress.

Having made sure that the artist is comfortable and suitably dressed, the work for the costume assistant will be organized so that the artist always has assistance, but any preparation and planning for another sequence can be done throughout the day. There should always be a costume assistant on set to take continuity notes and photographs between shots. There may be a continuity book where all these notes and photographs are recorded at the end of each day.

If the work is outdoors the assistant will need to have extra warm clothes available in between shots for artists and may be responsible for umbrellas to keep them dry.

On an ongoing production costumes need to be collected at the end of each day and prepared for morning or for the next time the costume is required. Naturally this means that the costume department are among the last to leave.

Costumes ready to be distributed to dressing rooms

Costume supervisor or assistant costume designer

A costume supervisor, sometimes known as an assistant costume designer, is a person with a great deal of experience in working in the media, who is able to take responsibility for the everyday running of a production. That may be as simple as contacting artists beforehand to suggest what clothes to bring with them and checking that all is well on the day, or it may mean organizing other staff needed in the department.

Their main responsibility is the running of the wardrobe department on a day-to-day basis. This will entail setting up the wardrobe department ahead, including checking the facilities available, and then maintaining the costumes and the continuity of the production. This is possibly a greater responsibility for costume than for other departments as artists may have several costumes in one day. Costume notes must be produced detailing changes, photos taken on a daily basis and entered into the continuity book. It is necessary to ensure that there are doubles of everything to cover for loss or damage. This includes any jewellery, and particular care must be taken if the artists are using their own jewellery. This is sometimes taken care of by the costume staff for the duration of the production.

An unusual game of cricket

Costume supervisors work alongside designers, so all the skills required for preparation of a production are needed, including:

- script breakdown and schedules;
- budgeting;
- continuity;
- liaising with other departments;
- speaking to artists;
- planning dress fittings and shopping;
- organizing other members of staff.

It is important to consider if the budget covers all eventualities. Even if the artist wears their own clothes the budget should cover spare clothes and clothes for doubles. Whenever there is a new costume worn for the first time it is important that the supervisor or designer is available. It may be that the costume is not suitable, for instance for lighting reasons, and that changes have to be made.

At the end of the production (or sooner, if no longer needed) clothes and jewellery that have been hired have to be returned, and it may be that some clothes can be sold to reduce the budget used.

Costume supervisor or assistant designer

Costume designer

A costume designer has sufficient knowledge and experience to take full responsibility for all production requirements. There may also be a costume supervisor and assistants responsible for the everyday running of the production while the designer concentrates on the designing or planning, buying, making and hiring of costumes. As with other heads of department, costume designers have to know how to research their subject and how and where to have costumes made or hired. As well as familiarity with large costumiers they will need to find 'costume makers' – people who may work from home making clothes specifically for productions.

On feature films there may be as many as 20 out-workers required, including milliners, and it is sometimes necessary that the 'workroom' stays with the production. That is, a workroom is set up and costume makers hired for the duration of the film production, making costumes as they go along. This may entail travelling, setting up a workroom at different locations.

In creating this alien it was decided that the scale effect of the costume could be made from the same foam latex as the face pieces

As with other designers, a costume designer joins a production some time before shooting starts to discuss the requirements and any problems that may arise. They may be required to produce drawings of designs and outfits for discussion with the producer or director. This can be very creative work, for example in designing costumes for a group of dancers, and it is extremely rewarding to see your work on camera.

Designers meet with the artists during rehearsals or before filming commences for dress fittings or to go shopping. Clothes for background artists, for doubles and for stunt doubles must also be prepared. Once shooting starts, keeping an eye on the production and constantly preparing for the days ahead require a great deal of organization and stamina!

In the theatre the costume designer often works very closely with the art director. They may be working to his or her overall design of the production. It is possible that the costume designer is asked to design costumes for a theatre production and, once made, their work is finished. The maintaining of the department may then be the responsibility of a supervisor who stays with the production.

Costume and make-up work together

Getting started

Make-up and hair

When beginning your career the first big outlay is buying stock and equipment in order to work. It is worth visiting a specialized supplier to see what is available and to get good advice. A full kit can take years to build up and will be expensive; there is no need to buy everything at once. It is important, though, to buy good quality tools – poor quality tools will make your work harder. A few sable-hair make-up brushes of different sizes, which can be cleaned properly, are much better value than many cheaper nylon brushes that would be harder to work with.

There will be many bags to carry, especially if carrying hairdressing equipment, and a set of wheels is a good investment. Good organization is necessary to avoid turning up at your location very early in the morning cluttered and stressed!

A make-up kit consists of many small items that should be well organized in some kind of box, again to make your work easy – when you are under time pressure you need to have everything to hand and know where everything is. To save expense, a fishing tackle box will suffice, but specialized make-up boxes are designed to hold the various pots, jars and brushes so are much better value in the end.

Having collected together a comprehensive kit you will need to develop a procedure of work.

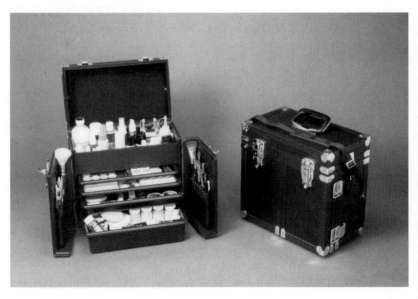

A professional make-up box, which can be placed on the bench beside you as you work

Having arrived early enough to set up before artists arrive, your make-up place needs to be prepared. If you have access to large rolls of tissue it is best to lay tissue on the bench before you start. This looks fresh and clean and can be replaced when necessary. It is useful to have a small kit box to hold materials needed for straightforward make-up, which can sit on the table next to you. There will not be a great deal of space and you will only want to have out the things that are being used. Pots for brushes and sponges are useful to save space and help you to know which brushes have been used and which are clean; as they are used they can be put on the table ready for cleaning. It is important that the artist can see that you are clean and well organized.

Having prepared your work site you are ready for introductions and to make your artist feel relaxed. Their clothes will need to be protected with a gown and, if doing make-up, a headband will be needed to keep their hair off the face.

If the hair has to be set in rollers it is usual to do this first. If there are two departments, hair and make-up, the order of work will need to be discussed and it is likely that make-up will take over once the hair is set.

Cleansing is the first important process. Even if the artist's skin is clean it is relaxing to have the face gently massaged with some cool toner on damp cotton wool.

You may have a specific make-up to do or you may want to discuss with the artist what they like themselves so that you can judge what is best for them. You should by now have a good routine in your work and it is sometimes helpful to talk about what you are doing as you go along. This makes the artist feel more involved in the work and gives them a chance to say how they feel and what they like.

Having completed the make-up the hair needs to be dressed. However, it is wise to check if the artist's costume is put on over the head. If it is not possible to dress first, a fine chiffon scarf placed over the completed hairstyle before pulling clothing over will help keep it intact.

Finally, having dressed, the make-up should be checked again. First, the make-up will have had time to settle and a little more powder may be needed and, second, the colouring of the costume and the dressed hair may mean adjustments to the colouring of the make-up.

Getting started

Costume

Costume staff also have to provide their own materials and equipment. This may mean providing ironing boards and irons as well as a comprehensive sewing kit. It is surprising what costume staff may be called on to 'fix' and tools such as small hammers, Stanley knives and pliers are necessary. Cleaning materials are essential, just as coloured sprays and powders, used for making clothes look dirty, and double-sided sticky tape is kept by every department! There is a product called Tessa Tape, which is a black foam sponge used for reducing noise, that is sometimes useful for the soles and heels of shoes. If working outdoors, towels and extra warm clothes may be needed.

It is necessary also for costume staff to set up before the artists arrive. Dressing rooms have to be found and ironing facilities readied. If the artists are bringing their own clothes these will have to be checked for colour suitability and any problems that might arise, such as making sure they can be fitted with a microphone.

On a larger production the costumes may have already been fitted and labelled and will need to be placed in the appropriate dressing rooms. It is usual that the make-up or hair is done before dressing, but sometimes artists check what they are wearing before anything else. It is also good to be able to introduce yourself at this stage and make sure you know when to be available to help.

While artists are in other departments there are usually lots of things to be organized by the costume personnel. There may be artists arriving a little later to be planned for, or changes of clothes to be readied. On an ongoing production there may be laundry from previous days to see to.

Whether the artist needs help dressing or not will depend on the costume of course, but the dressed artist will always need to have their clothes checked before any filming takes place. Most important will be continuity notes. Everything worn, including jewellery, will have to be listed with dates and scene numbers.

A make-up stool is useful for snatching minutes to study lines

Make-up and costume staff take a rest between shots and check notes

Getting work

Getting work in this business can be an extremely daunting prospect. You need to be resilient and not too fazed by rejection. There are many people trying to get work in this field and courage and perseverance are necessary.

The first thing is to get the best training you can find. There are many different college courses: media study, hairdressing and make-up, and courses in theatre costume and fashion design. They all offer a good grounding, and experience in being in a more adult environment. It is often difficult to get work before the age of twenty, as some maturity is necessary.

Time spent as a 'runner' with a film or TV production would be extremely useful. A runner is someone who does any little job necessary, mainly for the production team, but also for other departments. This work is extremely badly paid, if paid at all, but does give people the opportunity to experience this kind of work and the commitment required for it. It may be possible to do voluntary work in the department of your choice, just to get the experience. Such opportunities also give you the chance to get to know people and might lead to work eventually.

You will need a CV, or curriculum vitae, and you will also need to build up a portfolio of your work. College work will be a start.

Make-up

Some colleges offer courses in both hairdressing and make-up skills. This would be an ideal way to gain skills for TV and film work. Training as a beautician, either at college or with a make-up manufacturer, will provide some expertise but will not include any training in the effects of lighting and cameras.

There are shorter courses and workshops specific to film and TV work available. They should be investigated and if you can find one that has tutors with some experience of the business that is preferable.

Hairdressing

Hairdressing is still mainly learnt by taking a three-year apprenticeship with a hairdressing salon. This will give you a good knowledge and plenty of experience of working with hair. It takes time to become accomplished at managing hair well, more so than with other departments.

All aspects of hairdressing will be learnt, perming or straightening of hair, colouring hair, cutting and dressing of hair, and attaching false hair as in extensions. All this will enable you to work as an assistant hairdresser.

The different aspects of film work may have to be learnt as you go along. There may be short courses or workshops on period hairdressing, otherwise you will have to rely on the time and goodwill given by more experienced people.

Costume

Training should cover sewing skills and an understanding of the media and there are many college courses available for this. Even if the final goal is designing, knowledge of sewing and making clothes is necessary. There are also courses in fashion design; these are a necessary prerequisite if you wish to go on to be a costume designer. Sometimes people with art qualifications become costume designers.

Alternatively, having learnt to sew, a good place to get experience is at a costumiers. Here you can learn about making and fitting costumes.

Many people are content to work as dressers for productions. To get this work you need to be known to production or costume staff. If your sewing skills are very good, you can offer to help a designer with making or repairing costumes on a production. This may lead to regular employment and will certainly help build up a CV and portfolio.

Film colleges sometimes need help with their end-of-course film work, and it may be possible to get copies of the film to show potential employers.

Getting work

Kit

A comprehensive kit is collected over a long period of time and as a consequence of many different productions. The greater the responsibility the costume or make-up artist has, the bigger the kit will need to be. Obviously, the larger the kit, the more consideration needed as to how to transport it. A designer working on a large production will have many bags and boxes and will also need facilities at home for storage.

A small basic kit would comprise an appropriate box to hold small quantities of tools and products. Plastic toolboxes or fishing tackle boxes are often used but it is advisable to check the size of the compartments inside before buying. Boxes that have changeable compartments are best, so that they can be adapted to carry different products. There are specially designed make-up boxes, which are much better but, as they are also designed for travel and durability, they are expensive. As these boxes will contain many small items it is helpful if they can stand on a workbench while you are working because lack of space and time would not allow for everything to be unpacked.

A box or bag is necessary to hold the items that may be required on set. The make-up or wardrobe room may not have easy access to the studio or location. Some bags are designed to double as seats; there is a great deal of standing around while filming, and sitting on scenery or equipment is not advisable.

Whether you are working with make-up, hair or costume, there are some basic essentials that, after cleaning and maintaining, will remain packed ready for the next job. In addition to those, the requirements of each job will have to be considered to make sure all eventualities are catered for. Many of the items of a make-up kit will also be used by someone working with hair or costume, just as many make-up artists will also have hair equipment and some sewing kit.

Custom-made make-up boxes

Make-up

- *Cleanliness:* to present yourself well it is helpful to have something to lay your kit on, perhaps a towel or large sheet of tissue. Towels, wraps and hair bands to protect the artists' clothes and hair, water, soap and small bowls for water, cleaning fluids, etc. Cleansing, toning and moisturizing lotions and creams can be carried in smaller bottles to save space and weight. Cotton wool, cotton buds, tissues and wet wipes, cologne, chamois leather, barrier cream and deodorants.
- *Foundations:* a selection of liquid foundations in light, medium and dark shades, and the same for coloured skins. A similar selection of cream, grease and powder-based foundations, and some aquacolours. Light concealer creams. For coloured grease make-up for character work there are containers that hold small quantities instead of carrying all the sticks and pots around. Aquacolours.
- *Powder:* a fine translucent powder and one or two coloured powders, especially for coloured skins. A selection of pressed powder and several powder puffs of different sizes. Talcum powder.
- *Eye make-up:* a selection of coloured eye shadows, including natural beige and brown colours, as well as those with a heavy colour pigment designed for darker skins. Mascara in several colours. It is more hygienic for artists to use their own mascara wands but it is necessary to have some in your kit.

Kit

A bag that doubles as a seat

A selection of brushes

There are water-based mascaras that can be applied with a brush, which can then be washed. It is useful to have a water-resistant mascara as well. Eyebrow pencils. Eyeliners, eyelash dye and eyelash curlers. False eyelashes and adhesive.

- *Rouge or blushers:* several different makes and colours of blusher. They vary in colour pigment and heaviness of powder. Include light, natural brown colours, which are good for men. There are creams that give a very nice effect and are obviously applied before powder.
- *Lipsticks:* a selection of all colours. Instead of carrying around loose sticks they can be put into a container, so that you have a good selection of colours.
- *Sponges:* natural sponges, firm and soft stipple sponges for stippling colour onto skin, e.g. broken veins, freckles and bruises, and adding texture to wax and prosthetic modelling. A cheap foam baby sponge that can be cut up and discarded after use.
- *Brushes:* several sizes of sable-hair brushes, softer brushes for powder or blusher brushes, lipstick brushes and eyebrow brushes. An old toothbrush for cleaning hair lace and an eyelash comb or brush for separating lashes.
- *Nail products:* a selection of nail varnish colours. Varnish remover. Cuticle cream and clippers. Emery boards and cuticle sticks – useful for many things not just cleaning nails. Nailbrush. False nails and adhesive.
- *Electrical items:* electric shaver, shaving foam and razor. Clippers.
- *Spirits:* acetone, surgical spirit, methylated spirit, cleaning solvent for brushes, and Mastix Remover or spirit gum remover.

- *Special effects:* mortician's wax – soft and firm, modelling tools, latex, scar plastic, sealer, adhesives and remover, petroleum jelly and fuller's earth – useful for 'dirt' and breaking down. Glycerine and a tear stick. Crêpe hair and real hair – old beards and moustaches are useful. Coloured hair sprays.
- *Scissors:* for different uses including hairdressing scissors. Hair combs and brushes.
- *Also:* tong heater and selection of postiche tongs. Malleable block and pins. Double sided tape.

Hair

- A selection of combs and brushes for cutting, blow-drying and dressing hair.
- Electrical equipment: hairdryer, heated rollers, tongs – gas tongs are also useful, crimping and straightening tongs.
- Hairgrips and pins in all colours. Hair clips for setting hair.
- Shampoo, conditioner and hair products such as setting lotions, mousse and hair wax.
- Hair sprays for controlling hair and for colouring hair.

Costume

- Sewing box, needles, pins and threads of all colours and thicknesses. Scissors for different uses. Thimble. Wool and darning needles. Tailoring chalk. Double-sided tape. Buttons and fasteners, safety pins.
- Tools: various tools are often required for costumes and shoes. Hammer, wire cutters, pliers and Stanley knives.
- Anti-shine spray, talcum powder, fuller's earth, petroleum jelly and coloured sprays, all useful for breaking down clothes.
- Washing materials: soaps and towels, washing powders and softener, dry cleaning fluids and stain removers. Bowls, cotton wool and tissues. Deodorants.
- Iron and board, water spray and spray starch.
- Clothes brush.
- Dressing gowns for artists while changing. Spare thermal underclothes and T-shirts for warmth.

Kit

Side effects

Most products have been well tested, but it is as well to know the dangers of the products you use. Products for external use only should never be ingested. You should also be aware that there is always some absorption through the skin of all products, regardless of toxicity. It is advisable always to wear protective gloves.

Aerosol sprays
Aerosol sprays, by the millions, have been used in the home, as cosmetics and in industry for decades now. In the make-up business they are mostly used for hair lacquers, deodorants and perfumes. If used as instructed they rarely cause problems but the fine vapour can get into the lungs and irritate lung tissue. Asthma and other respiratory difficulties may be triggered, as well as infections and allergic reactions. Water-soluble lacquers are less harmful, both to people and the environment. Great care should always be taken, especially with children. It helps if a tissue or towel is held over the mouth and nose.
   Aerosol spray cans are highly inflammable and should always be disposed of carefully.

After-shave
After-shave contains perfume and alcohol, mainly as ethyl alcohol. It can cause irritation to sensitive skins.

Alcohol
Ethyl alcohol is used as a solvent in many products. If swallowed it can cause a drop in blood sugar levels that can lead to fits.
   Perfumes, toilet water and cosmetics may contain up to 40 per cent alcohol.
   Benzene products have been removed from solvents. They have been replaced with Toluene, which is methyl-Benzene. This is safer although still toxic. Tetrachlorethylene is the usual solvent in dry cleaning products and, if inhaled, may lead to liver or renal dysfunction. Fluid in the lungs has also been associated with its inhalation. All such products should be used sparingly and with caution.

Carbon tetrachloride
This dry cleaning solvent is toxic even in small quantities and has been removed from most household products. There are less toxic dry cleaning fluids available now. The main side effects of inhalation are headaches, gastrointestinal irritation with nausea, a sore throat and temperature, and it can cause heart dysfunction and liver damage.

Correction fluid

Trichloroethane is the solvent used in correction fluid and thinners. Drug abusers, especially teenagers, often inhale it. It is highly inflammable and toxic. It is a central nervous system depressant. Excessive use may cause headaches and drowsiness.

Cosmetics

Side effects are mostly skin irritations and allergies. Some cosmetics contain ammonia, acetic acid and trichloroethylene, which can cause redness, itching and sometimes swelling. The sensitivity and age of the skin affect susceptibility and open wounds may develop. Perm products, depilatory creams and cuticle removers are particular culprits. Conjunctivitis can be caused by cosmetics and nails can be damaged. Perfume in antiperspirants can cause irritation.

The main difficulty is that it can take up to 48 hours for a reaction to take place, which could lead to uncertainty as to which cosmetic was the cause. Once a sensitizing reaction has occurred, continued use of that cosmetic will cause an increasingly severe reaction. An allergic reaction can suddenly occur after years of untroubled use.

Exposure to sunlight may aggravate a reaction to cosmetic products, especially the perfume added to them during manufacture.

The chemicals widely used are acetic acid, amyl acetate, acetone, aluminium chloride, pyrimidine and thioglycolic acid. Other substances that can cause allergy are formaldehyde, balsam of Peru, cocoa butter, lanolin and fragrances.

Deodorants and antiperspirants

As well as the effects caused by the aerosols, skin reactions are quite frequent. They should never be used on damaged skin or sensitive genital skin. They can cause irritations and rashes.

Detergents

Household detergents are less irritating than commercial products, but can still be highly alkaline. They can cause breathing difficulties if inhaled, especially in infants.

Disinfectants

These may contain chloropheno-, chloroxyleno-, isopropyl and other phenolic alcohol. Isopropyl alcohol has twice the toxicity of ethyl alcohol because it is converted into acetone within the body.

Irritation of the throat, mouth and gastrointestinal tract can occur, as can depression of the nervous system, causing drowsiness and coma. A very large overdose could cause kidney failure.

Bleach contains chlorine-based components.

Methyl alcohol (Methanol)

This is more toxic then ethyl alcohol as it forms formaldehyde within the body. It is widely used in antifreeze, paint remover and varnish.

Symptoms are nausea, vomiting, abdominal pain and headaches. It can produce a fall in blood pressure and visual damage leading to blindness.

Methylated spirit

This actually contains only 5 per cent of methyl alcohol (see above). Its main danger is the ethyl alcohol. Misuse will, of course, also have the effects of methyl alcohol.

Nail varnish and remover

Nail varnish may contain acetone and amyl acetate, both products subjects of drug abuse. Remover will almost certainly contain acetone. Most dangerous is sniffing acetone or nail varnish remover.

Perfumes

These are a mixture of essential oils and alcohol, mainly ethyl alcohol. Unless swallowed, the main reaction would be skin irritation and rashes.

Portable gas fires and burners

These burn butane or propane gas and give off carbon monoxide fumes if not functioning properly. Carbon monoxide is poisonous and can be fatal. Fires should be regularly maintained and used in well-ventilated rooms.

The main symptoms are headaches, dizziness, confusion, nausea, vomiting and respiratory failure. Heart problems can also occur.

Shampoo

Unless swallowed, when they cause mild stomach upsets, shampoos are mostly non-toxic.

Shellac

This is an unsaturated polyester resin derived from the hardened secretion of the lac insect. There are two grades of shellac that contain wax and two that do not. A wax-free, refined, bleached shellac is used in cosmetics and hair lacquers. It appears to be not very toxic but may cause skin allergy.

Surgical spirit

This contains ethyl alcohol. As before, unless swallowed, so causing low blood sugar levels and the possibility of fits, it may cause skin irritation.

Talcum powder (hydrated magnesium silicate)

Talcum powder may contain magnesium and aluminium silicate, which can enter the body through the skin pores where it may set up a chronic inflammation with painful localized irritation.

Generally adverse skin reaction is mild, but the product should always be used with care after cosmetic shaving or hair removal.

Washing powders and liquids

As with shampoos, the main problem is if the foam is inhaled. Washing-up liquids may contain some alcohol but are not highly toxic.

Washing materials and equipment should always be rinsed thoroughly before the item is dried.

Side effects

Glossary

Acetone   commonly used for removing nail varnish, but also used for cleaning hair lace; *never* used directly on skin; available from chemists.
Adhesive   different types are used for sticking wig hair lace, eyelashes, prosthetics, etc.; available from theatrical suppliers and chemists.
Alginate   mixed into a jelly-like substance used for making life casts; available from dental suppliers.
Aquacolour   a water-soluble compressed powder foundation used in character make-up.
Artificial eyelashes   for extra emphasis on the eyes; available in different lengths and thicknesses; can be trimmed; applied with adhesive.

Backcombing   a technique used to make hair appear fuller than it is.
Bald caps   specially made plastic caps to simulate a bald head.
Blending   the technique of working-in make-up so that colours pass imperceptibly into each other and to eradicate hard edges where make-up meets skin.
Block   a minimally modelled head made from a variety of materials; used in wig making and dressing; available from hairdressing suppliers.
Blocking, as in rehearsal   the first meeting of artists and director to block the moves that will be made on set.
Blocking a wig   securing a wig on a block with galloon, a tape to protect the hair lace or to dress the wig.
Blow-drying   a technique of drying the hair, lifting and styling with the hairbrush.
Breaking down   a special effects make-up or costume for specific actions or locations, e.g. poverty, war, coal mine.
Brightness   the amount of light or dark in a colour or picture.

Call sheets   the daily instructions for the following day's work, giving times artists will be called and scene and location details.
Camera tests   a chance to see someone on camera for an audition or prior to filming.
Camouflage make-up   a high-pigment make-up for covering skin imperfections.
Chamois leather   a soft leather cloth, often soaked in cologne and used for cooling artists.
Chroma key   a technical operation of superimposing a foreground subject onto a completely different background.
Cleaning fluid   used for cleaning wigs or costumes.
Colour temperature   the amount of brightness in a colour or picture.
Compact powders   available in a variety of colours, shiny or matt; include eyeshadow, blushers or rouge; available from make-up suppliers.
Continuity   ensuring consistency in production by matching make-up, hair, costume and props to each linked scene.

Costumiers a place where a large stock of costumes are kept for hiring or buying.

Doubles extra artists used as 'stand ins', usually for stunt scenes; extra clothes or wigs required for 'stand ins' to match the artist's appearance exactly.
Drawing mats used in the making of wigs for holding hair ready for knotting.
Dressing hair styling natural hair or wigs to create appropriate effects; a variety of tools and techniques are used.

Extras walk-on artists, used for background interest.

Face powder used to set the foundation and reduce shine; loose or compact; available in different colours.
Fantasy make-up to create a non-natural look; a free-style make-up used in a range of fantasy productions.
Foundation face the base upon which colour is built up to achieve the desired effect.
Foundation wig the net into which hair is knotted.
French pleat a technique of dressing hair up from off the shoulders.

Gallery an area in the studio where the technical and production staff watch the pictures from the various cameras and make adjustments.
Gel a transparent plastic material in many different colours used as light filters.
Gelatine used in make-up for small-scale special effects and prosthetics.
Glycerine a slow-moving liquid sometimes mixed with water and used to simulate sweat and tears; available from chemists.

Hackle a tool used in wig making for combing and mixing loose hair.
Hair, human used for fine wigs and to provide body for wigs.
Hair, crêpe used for fun wigs and to provide body for wigs.
Hair, yak a coarser animal hair used for facial and body hair pieces.
Hair lace the net into which hair is knotted; also known as a ventilating net.
Heated rollers an electrical appliance to heat rollers for setting hair.
Highlighting using a light colour to emphasize a feature.

Knotting technique of attaching hair to hair lace.
Knotting hooks tools used in wig making for attaching hair to the foundation.

Latex a natural rubber of various densities used in special effects make-up, e.g. wrinkles, wounds, burns, bald caps.
Laying on hair the application of loose hair directly to the body.
Life cast taking an exact impression of a face or body part, which is then replicated in a mould.
Live transmission when something is broadcast directly to the audience as it happens.

Glossary

Modelling   building and sculpting features for prosthetic work.

Modelling materials   clay, plasticine, wax; available from pottery and artists' suppliers, and from make-up suppliers.

Modelling tools   a variety of tools used in modelling; standard sculpting tools and dentists' tools are useful.

Modelling with wax   working directly on the face or body to build up or change the shape of a feature using wax.

Monitors   television screens showing the selected pictures.

Mortician's wax   the material used in direct application to alter features, e.g. nose, ears, chin; also used for blocking out eyebrows.

OB   outside broadcast; where the technical vans go to the location of the production such as a theatre or sports centre.

Out-workers   people who do specific work at home, such as wig and costume makers.

Pancake   a grease-free cake make-up; generally used for covering large areas.

Panstick   a grease make-up commonly used for character make-up.

Pencils   wooden pencils with soft grease 'leads' used for colouring eyebrows and outlining eyes and lips.

Plaster of Paris   used for making positive and negative prosthetic moulds; available from chemists, dental and artists' suppliers.

Plastic   used in liquid form for making bald caps and prosthetics; available from theatrical make-up suppliers.

Plasticine   modelling material used in prosthetic work; does not dry out as does clay; available from artists' and make-up suppliers.

Postiche   the name given to knotted or woven hair pieces of various shapes and sizes; used for adding to wigs or hair to create different hairstyles.

Powder brush   a soft brush used for removing excess powder.

Quick changes   a moment in the recording or transmission when changes can be made to costume and make-up, often with very little time.

Rehearse/record   when a production can be broken into scenes or sections and each section rehearsed immediately prior to recording; done for production purposes as well as for the sake of the artists.

Run through   a rehearsal for all departments to see the action and the shots.

Runner   a person available to give general help on a production; usually a student and usually assigned to the production department.

Running order   a document showing the order of recording or transmission, giving such details as artists required, time and shots.

Rushes   the roll of film, once completed, is 'rushed' to be roughly edited ready to be viewed the next day.

Sealer a thin plastic product designed to seal effects before applying make-up.

Script breakdown each department examines the script to identify different requirements depending on the time and location of the action.

Shading using a dark colour to lessen the impact of a feature.

Spirit gum the most commonly used adhesive in attaching wig lace, bald caps, etc.; available from make-up suppliers.

Standing by being available near artists on set to touch-up if required.

Stipple sponge a firm sponge with larger holes designed to create a textured effect with make-up.

Straight make-up the application of make-up to delineate and enhance the face and to correct imperfections.

Strobe the effect caused when a small pattern causes the picture to break up as the camera angle changes.

Stubble paste in stick form, used on the face before applying tiny hairs to create beard stubble.

Surgical spirit a useful cleaning fluid for removing spirit gum.

T-pins used to attach wigs to blocks; available from hairdressing suppliers.

Tone the amount of brightness in colour.

Tongs metal, scissor-like tool for creating curls and waves.

Tongs heater an electric heater for heating up iron tongs.

Tooth enamel a varnish applied to teeth to discolour them.

Toupee a hairpiece made specifically for a man to cover his balding head; attached with clips or double-sided toupee tape.

Transmission lights blue and red lights immediately outside the studio; a flashing red light signals that recording is taking place and no entry is allowed.

Video assist film cameras can be linked to a small video monitor to enable staff to see pictures being filmed.

Wig stand to hold a wig block while dressing; either free-standing or can be clamped to a work bench or table.

Witch hazel a natural toning lotion for the skin.

Glossary

Further reading

Baker, Patricia (1993). *Wigs and Make-up for Theatre, TV and Film.* Butterworth-Heinemann.

Baygan, Lee (1984). *Make-up for Theatre and Television.* A&C Black.

Baygan, Lee (1988). *Techniques of Three-Dimensional Make-up.* Watson-Guptill.

Black, J.Anderson, Garland, Madge and Kennett, Frances (1980). *The History of Fashion.* Orbis

Bradfield, Nancy (1981). *Costume In Detail: Women's Dress 1730–1930.* Harrap.

Bradfield, Nancy (1995). *Historical Costume of England from the 11th Century to the 20th Century.* E. Dobby.

Buchman, Herman (1973). *Film and Television Make-up.* Watson-Guptill.

Buchman, Herman (1989). *Stage Make-up.* Watson-Guptill.

Corson, Richard (1972). *Fashion in Make-up.* Peter Owen.

Corson, Richard (1986). *Stage Make-up.* Peter Owen.

Corson, Richard (1991). *Fashion in Hair.* Peter Owen.

Delama, Penny (1995). *The Complete Make-up Artist.* Macmillan.

Green, Martin, Palladino, Leo and Kimber, Lesley (2000). *Professional Hairdressing*, third edition. Thomson Learning.

Kehoe, Vincent (1991). *Special Make-up Effects.* Focal Press.

Kehoe, Vincent (1995). *The Technique of the Professional Make-up Artist.* Focal Press.

Laver, James (1963). *Costumes Through the Ages: 1000 Illustrations.* Thames & Hudson Ltd.

Laver, James (1969). *Costume and Fashion: A Concise History.* Thames & Hudson Ltd.

Nunn, Juan (1990). *Fashion in Costume 1200–1980.* Herbert Press.

Palladino, Leo (1989). *The Principles and Practice of Hairdressing.* Macmillan.

Palladino, Leo (1991). *Hairdressing – The Foundations.* Macmillan.

Ribero, Aileen, Cumming, Valerie (1989). *The Visual History of Costume.* B.T. Batsford Ltd.

Schick, I.T. (1983). *Uniforms of the Worlds Great Armies – 1700 to present.* Peerage.

Wilcox, R.Turner (1959). *The Mode in Hats and Headdresses, Including Hair Styles, Cosmetics and Jewelry.* Charles Scribner's Sons.